M000226325

demystifying
COLLEGE
ADMISSIONS

UPDATED MARCH 2019

TERRY GREENE CLARK

Copyright © 2019 by Terry Greene Clark

All rights reserved. This book or any portion thereof (except where otherwise noted on the page) may not be reproduced or used in any manner whatsoever without the express written permission of the publisher except for the use of brief quotations in a book review.

Cover image © Bryan Harris | Dreamstime.com

Printed in the United States of America

Revised edition, first printing, 2019

ISBN 978-0-9964739-3-4

www.terrygreeneclark.com

contents

preface

The realization of this book has truly been a journey. In retrospect, the seeds may have been planted long ago when my mother, after reading my fifth grade book report declared, "You have a way with words." Although this praise stuck with me throughout the years and I continued to enjoy research and writing in high school and college, it never occurred to me that I could write as a hobby or even a profession. It wasn't until I was married with three toddlers under the age of five that I realized there were a lot of stories rolling around in my head. Occasionally, I could get them down on paper but raising three and then four children did not leave me with much time to write. When my oldest daughter, Aly, went off to college in 2011, I started sending her long letters full of family stories and "pearls of wisdom." She loved reading them and that encouragement awoke in me a sleeping giant. I became a closet writer, composing letters to my children, and writing short stories and poems about my life experiences as a Mom. I never shared them with anyone, not even my husband, but thought maybe someday, I might.

So you can imagine my amazement when I found myself on a flight from Charlotte to Boston in June of 2012, sitting next to motivational speaker and author Simon T. Bailey, openly discussing my idea for this book. (Simon Bailey is the author of *Release Your Brilliance* and several other books.) I was returning to Boston from a multi-state, Southern college road trip with my son, Patrick, and Simon was flying to Boston to speak at a forum at the Hynes Auditorium. Simon was very friendly and struck up a conversation with me. As we spoke, I discovered that we had many things in common. We spoke at length about the college matriculation process since this had been my second time experiencing it.

As our dialogue progressed, I finally got the nerve to say out loud to Simon, a perfect stranger, what I had been thinking about for some time. I said, "With all the schools I have visited and information I have learned about how college admissions works, I should write a book about the college process for parents." His response - "You should do it. " He added that it was a renewable topic that could be updated and would make a great EBook. I read his *Release Your Brilliance* book that summer and it, in part, inspired me to seriously pursue this suppressed dream of writing. That summer I outlined the entire book and wrote the first two chapters. As the demands of family and life tugged at me, my dream took a back seat to my responsibilities. Throughout the rest of 2012 and 2013, I was able to work on bits and pieces of this book, but nothing substantial. In 2014 as I prepared to send yet another child off to college, I took more notes and delved further into this mysterious process of applying to college. In September of 2014, I made a commitment that completing this book would be my job everyday while the kids were at school. Today, you hold in your hand, a book I dared to write and publish. It symbolizes a new life purpose for myself.

It may seem strange that it has taken me this long to get to a point that I not only recognize what I want to do but believe that this is what I was meant to do. I realize that my life experiences up until this point prepared me for this new beginning. I needed to be a daughter, a sister, a businesswoman, a wife, a mother and a friend in order to become a thoughtful and honest author. I hope you find this book helpful and that it may inspire you in other ways.

acknowledgments

The African Proverb, "It takes a village to raise a child," is a sentiment I have always embraced, but I discovered that this saying is also applicable to the realization of this book; it took the knowledge of a village to help me write it. It is in this spirit that I offer my heart-felt thanks to all who have influenced me over the years and have helped to make this book a reality.

My four children, Aly, Patrick, Tora and Reece, my life's work, who have not only inspired me but have freely given me permission to share their stories with you throughout this book.

My husband, Greg, who has always supported and encouraged me throughout our entire marriage, but also affirmed his love and commitment to me and this project every day by ignoring the fact that most of my other responsibilities went by the wayside during this time.

My mother, Mary Greene Dwyer, and father-in-law and mother-in-law, Richie and Pat Clark, who raised six children each in a family atmosphere that promoted love, honesty, loyalty and hard work.

My sisters, sister in laws, brothers, brother in laws, nieces and nephews whose love, support and relationships I treasure. Your candor and honesty enabled me to provide a more in depth explanation and a reality check for this project.

Simon T. Bailey, whose affirmation of my dream and book, *Release Your Brilliance*, gave me the courage to share my stories with you. His willingness to impart his knowledge, information and resources provided me with a solid foundation to tackle the world of publishing.

Caroline Bartholomew, the editor, whose competence and calm, steady hand made this book more consistent and much easier to read.

Kate Binder, the graphic designer, whose work and patience helped me find the vision I wished to illustrate.

My dear friends who have been my advisors and cheerleaders. Kira Nelson and Eileen Forman who provided critical feedback on the first draft. Their detailed suggestions helped me to shape this book. Nikki Davis whose spirit and energy encouraged me to write. Bonnie Berg whose intellect and positive feedback always made me think. Melanie Kelly who, for many years, has been my confidant and sounding board in all things related to parenting, motherhood and college.

To all my many other wonderful friends who I have spent time discussing the college process over coffee or lunch, at Lighthouse Beach or on a walk around the neighborhood. The wisdom you shared contributed to this book. making me a better listener and writer.

introduction

I f you search "college admissions" on any reference website, thousands of titles appear offering expert advise on a myriad of themes related to admissions, but few specifically offer parents a simple guide, practical advice and real world experience. This single book will bring together all the information you need to know about the college application and matriculation process. This one resource will enable you to overcome the trepidation you feel about the illusiveness of higher education and gain control of the college search process for yourself and your student. It will equip you, the parent, with not only a road map of the college enrollment process, but also an explanation of the terminology, expectations and structure of this operation. The facts, simple steps and resources will empower you to take an active role in this process and help your student find the colleges that are the best fit.

In addition, this book provides a glimpse into my personal experience of having sent three teenagers off to college in six years. The individual journey of these three, dynamic young adults, exactly two years and three months apart, raised in the same home, by the same parents, gives this book a unique perspective on the college process. In the "Reality Check" parts of the book, I have chronicled the ups, downs, successes and missteps that occurred along the way with my own children as well as many nieces, nephews and sons and daughters of friends. It is my hope that this personal information will give you a practical understanding of what to expect during the whole college process.

This book focuses on the key information you need to know as a parent, while also identifying the nuances of the college process that exist at every turn. It will empower you to believe that the college process is not a passive experience that happens to you and your student. This book will arm you with knowledge and a realistic vision of the process, enabling both you and your student to take control and find the colleges that are the "best fit," both academically and financially.

> Due to the nature of this subject, College Admissions, and the dynamic features of the internet, there will inevitably be changes to policies, procedures and website addresses referenced in this book. For major developments, please refer to the "Updates" tab on my website, **www.terrygreeneclark.com**.

to it. My only life raft in this situation was hope. I was holding onto the hope that something productive would come out of this meeting I had requested with her college advisor because Aly and I were not on the same page and couldn't even seem to get the process started. I thought back to the days when potty training was the biggest worry on my plate. I remembered the wise words of an old friend: "No one goes to kindergarten in diapers. They all figure it out when they want to." I took a deep breath, relaxed and kept an open mind as our meeting progressed.

Ms. G had been an advisor at Weston High School for about six years. I am assuming she had seen this parent/child stalemate situation before because she smiled and calmly guided us to a solution. She listened to both of us argue our points and then said: "Okay. Pick a place to start." She had talked to Aly about some schools and their locations previously, so she directed us to the area of Virginia/DC/Maryland. Both Aly and I looked at each and shook our heads in agreement. Eureka!!! We had a starting point!

I would love to tell your that our college search was smooth from there on, but that would be a lie. Little did I know when I left Ms. G's office that the real work for Aly and me in finding the right school was yet to come. Since we did finally have a geographical area to explore, we were actually able to calmly communicate both our ideas and expectations of what an ideal college would be. The only criteria we could work with that fit Aly's requirements at the time were that there be a liberal arts program, that the school be located preferably in the Southern region of the U.S. and that it have a crew team. We both agreed to come up with universities that fit those standards and take the first week of the summer to go on a college road trip. We were off!

In subsequent weeks, I discovered that evaluating which colleges to visit could be a part- time or even a full- time job. Beginning the process of funneling the scope of schools involved much more time and research than I had anticipated. Another wise friend with credentials in the child psychology field told me: "Most 17-year-olds are not mature enough to execute this college process alone. They need help and guidance from their parents in order to make solid decisions." (Of course, this made me feel so much better about myself and my child because I thought I had the only 17-year-old who couldn't figure this stuff out.) Finding the U.S. Women's Rowing College list, determining which schools had Division I, II or III crew teams and whether the liberal arts program was strong, discovering basic logistical characteristics that, say, an urban versus a suburban campus would offer as well as factoring in the total size of the student body and the level of entrance difficulty were important steps to address in our decision making process. Even though I felt I knew what was best for Aly, I recognized that it was not my choice to make. If her college selection and ultimate college experience was going to be successful, she needed to see a variety of schools in order to make some of her own decisions and know what was the right fit for her. If I had told her I knew what was best for her, she might have acquiesced, but I knew there would come a time when she would doubt that and then even blame me for forcing her to go the way I thought was right. In order to grow, she needed to make some big decisions and maybe even some big mistakes on her own.

With the large number of schools we were talking about visiting and all of those pertinent factors to deal with, I decided I needed to create an Excel spreadsheet to keep track of everything in order to stay organized. (I must admit, I only made that spreadsheet with my first child. Having gone through the college process with my third child, a spreadsheet was something I would not even consider. That first child who goes off to college really does have to witness the neurotic side of their parents!) As the focus narrowed with our criteria in place, Aly and I were able to have calm, adult conversations about the schools that made the cut. She subsequently took the list and did some online research of her own, returning with an even shorter list of possibilities. I, in turn, looked at the geography of the chosen colleges and mapped out a road trip that had us visiting two institutions a day! We crisscrossed Virginia, DC and Maryland that week in June, but did we find the perfect college fit for Aly? I am sorry to say that, no, we did not. But we did come away with not only a clearer picture of what Aly wanted but also a better understanding of what needed to be done in order to make the most informed decisions at this point in the process.

I feel that this is an important time to say that it is never a waste of time to visit a college because you always learn something new on every trip. Even if students visit a school and despise it, they learn why. By articulating the pros and cons of an institution, they are making important distinctions and understanding where their interests lie. This realization helps narrow the options bringing more clarity to their visions. I also would like to reiterate the point that exploring a university does not necessarily require a plane ticket or a week away from work. A day trip on a Saturday or Sunday to a local university is just as helpful in getting your teenager to think more critically about college. This is especially true at the beginning of the process. Exploring a college you may pass everyday on the way to work, just with your child or on a guided tour if available, is a great way to get a feel for university life. Who is there on a Saturday? Is the library quiet or overcrowded? Are the buildings and grounds clean and up to date? How far apart are the classrooms? Does the campus feel safe? How far away are *you from the city, public transportation or any local businesses? Answering these questions will help you and your student understand what details matter and provide you both with a tangible feel for the college. Documenting the answers to those questions in a notebook and assessing them will be the key to helping your students weigh preferences and ultimately choose where they would enjoy studying.*

One of the most important lessons I learned on our college road trip was an understanding of why Aly felt so strongly about having a sports team in her college life. She had only started rowing as a junior in high school so I did not know whether it was even feasible for her to be a part of a college team. Furthermore, I did not understand why she would want to get up every morning at five to row in the cold. Little did I know that crew had become a way for her to cope with the social and stress-ridden situations that come with being a teenager. I had not realized how much it grounded her, giving her routine, balance, time management and social skills, friendships and joy. Crew had been her life line and allowed her to get through some difficult high school years. While driving through hundreds of miles of corn fields in Virginia, our discussion about why crew came to a head. In sheer frustration at my lack of understanding, Aly shouted: "I need it to survive! I need to know I will have friends and be able to do something I love! I need it to make sure I can survive college!" Aha! My dimwitted brain finally saw the light. Crew gave her confidence and strength to face the unknown. She was scared and recognized she needed the security and familiarity of that sport to help her succeed in college—a very mature insight for someone I had thought was not yet ready for college. To say the least, we never had that conversation again, and crew availability became one of the key factors in determining if a college was the right fit for Aly.

The reality is there are several colleges out there for every student. Believe it. Repeat it to yourself over and over again. Let it offer you comfort on those long difficult days of uncertainty. Know that statement is true. I used to believe that the only people who said that and meant it were the ones whose children had already been accepted into prestigious institutions. I was convinced they were just saying that to make everyone else feel better, but now I see the truth in it. By listening and focusing on what was really important to each of my three children regarding their higher education, the depth and breadth of our options narrowed. We were ultimately able to focus on what was the best fit for each of them, ensuring successful college careers.

beginning the process

STEP #1

Freshman Year: Do not do anything about the college search process at this point.

Let students explore who they are. Let them be young and not full of worry about the future.

STEP #2

Sophomore Year: Help your children focus on maintaining or getting good grades.

Encourage them to discover interests and commit to at least one sport and one or two clubs they might want to continue being a part of throughout high school.

STEP #3

Junior Year: Prepare for the most academically difficult and stressful year of high school.

Recognize that ramped up academics, taking the SAT/ACT, visiting colleges, appointments with college counselors, drafting a résumé and evaluating if they want to and are able to play college sports are just a few of the challenges your teenagers will face this year.

STEP #4

Senior Year: Prepare yourself and your students for a year full of decisions and changes.

Guiding your seniors through choices, developing "what if" scenarios, helping them develop a plan for meeting deadlines and following up on meetings and applications is what your students need from you this year.

Overview

Each of your children is unique, and, likewise, their interest in the college search process will vary. While there are many schools of thought on when students should begin looking and applying to colleges, most high school counselors seem to agree that junior year is the best starting point. Are there factors you should consider with your children before then? Absolutely! The following is a collection of ideas gathered from experiences my family and friends have had with their children during high school.

Freshman Year

Since the first year of high school is already full of angst, your child's freshman year should be all about focusing on adjusting to a new school environment. This is the year they are busy acclimating to rigorous academics, adjusting to a new social environment, learning more about themselves as individuals, exploring clubs or sports and finding the place where they feel comfortable and fit in. College should not be in the forefront of the student's or the parent's minds. The best gift you can give your freshman children is to help them develop a sense of themselves. When they understand who they are, confidence will shine through and strengths will surface. This will translate into not only success in high school but also will help them when it comes time to make decisions about college. Spending time talking to your students, building them up and helping them discover interests and strengths are what will pay off in the future. Social and peer pressure begin to play an important role in the lives of freshmen. Dealing with all of these changes is difficult enough for new high school students without the added stress of considering thoughts of college. Allow your students time to be 14 or 15 without worrying about the future.

NOTE: Parents may hear about subject tests, a standardized test offered to students on over 35 different subjects. Many top tier colleges who require subject tests as a component of the admissions application demand the scores from ALL tests to be submitted to the university. Chatter about subject tests is most common in the math and science arena because subjects, such as physics, are taught at different times depending upon local high schools. This matter is important because most high schools do not teach all the material covered on the exam so students often have to study independently in order to do well.

REALITY CHECK

Since many adults do not know what they want in life, it is easy to understand why freshmen are still unsure of themselves. In high school, students usually prefer to fly under the radar and just fit in. It is unfortunate in today's world that by the time most teens reach high school, they are already vested and focused on certain sports and clubs and too committed or nervous to try something new. What is holding them back? I think fear. They are afraid they will be embarrassed if they are not good enough. Alternatively, there are a small percentage of teens that are risk takers for the thrill of it and may try something new just because their friends are doing it. In order to strike a balance between the two, freshman year is a good time for parents to encourage students to be adventurous but in a way that promotes self-awareness and fun, not peer pressure and unnecessary risk.

When Victoria started high school in a community where she did not know one person, she was nervous but eager to make new friends. In order to broaden her sports horizons and develop a new circle of friends, she decided to try volleyball for the first time as a freshman because many of her middle school peers were going to play in high school. We supported her decision to do so and even sent her to a summer camp to prepare for it. As first semester progressed, Victoria did play JV volleyball and formed good friendships but she realized she just did not like volleyball as an organized sport. After talking to us about it, Victoria chose not to play the next year. (But the experience did make her want to try out for basketball – a real passion of hers and which she subsequently played all four years in high school.) I believe this experience taught her to step outside of her comfort zone but also listen to her own internal compass and what truly made her happy, without the influence of friends or outside forces.

Sophomore Year

I know many of you will doubt my advice on this but the best thing a sophomore can do is focus on getting good grades. One of the determining factors on any student's college application is GPA (grade point average). Most universities categorize students according to a weighted GPA. (A weighted GPA includes Science, English, Mathematics, History, and Language courses. Electives such as Drama, Art, Photography or Theology may not be included.) Many colleges have minimum grade point average requirements or a range of GPA scores they are willing to accept from students seeking admission. Most high schools do not calculate GPAs until a student has had two full years at that one institution. Therefore, the first GPA parents often see for their students may well be at the end of sophomore year. If, at that time, your student is disappointed in the bottom line, do not fret. Colleges like for grades to have an upward trajectory over the four years of high school because it shows improvement and mastery as students adjust to a more difficult curriculum. An additional factor that college admissions teams take into consideration when evaluating applicants' GPA scores is advanced placement and honors classes, most of which are not available until junior year.

Sophomore year is a good time for students to continue to explore new clubs or sports, but by the end of the first semester, they should be settled into at least one or two sports or clubs that they plan on being active members of for the rest of their high school experiences. Colleges like to see commitment to an activity for more than one year. If your child is an athlete, sophomore year is a good time for him or her to think about whether to play a sport recreationally or competitively in college. If there is interest in participating in top tier college sports—Division I or II—students probably need to make sure they attend certain tournaments or forums in order to get exposure to college coaches.

The Preliminary Scholastic Aptitude Test (PSAT) should be taken once by the spring of sophomore year. Many high schools administer the tests themselves. The American College Testing (ACT) offers a new student readiness assessment system called ACT Aspire. States, districts and schools can request these tests in order to help evaluate students. For more information, go to www.discoveractaspire.org.

Students should not worry about studying for preliminary tests since they are merely a measure of what they know at that point in time. These preliminary standardized tests serve several purposes. First, they help students get used to taking a lengthy, four-hour test while giving them the opportunity to understand how they could have done better or approached the tests differently. They can also be a guide to help students understand what they should focus on when preparing for the SAT/ACT in the future.

The gift of time for sophomores to be themselves, worry free, is the best gift parents can give. Let them learn who they are. Let them get to know their strengths and weaknesses. Encourage them. Listen to them. Guide them. Protect them.

REALITY CHECK

It is important to understand that there may be opportunities for your students to be exposed to a college setting in a non-threatening way if they are ready. Many clubs and athletic teams offer the opportunity to visit college campuses for tournaments or camps. These informal visits during sophomore and early junior years can be used to explore a specific institution or just to get a feel as to whether or not your child likes the size, geography or location of a given campus. If this situation presents itself, ask if your child wants to take an independent tour of the campus while there. If the

answer is "NO," honor that. If the student is eager or ambivalent, then go ahead, have lunch in the dining hall, look at the sports facilities, talk about the geographic location. You may be surprised at what you discover. Also, if there is an opportunity for younger children to visit colleges with an older sibling, it can also be a stress-free opportunity to expose them to the college world. Again, as long as your sophomore is agreeable to exploring, these informal visits can be a way to take some of the mystery and fear out of the college search process by allowing students to relax and enjoy being on college campuses before having to make major decisions.

I actually did take both of my rising sophomores on college road trips with their older siblings. In both cases, they enjoyed the exposure and ultimately thought these colleges would be among their top choices. When they became seniors, though, and were making their actual college selections, neither one of them chose to apply to those schools they had visited as sophomores. Their sophomore selves were very different from their senior selves. Does that mean it was a waste of time for them to come along on the road trips? In my experience, I would say no because it gave each of them a base of knowledge and a starting point for the future in a stress-free, non-threatening environment. Thank goodness they had evolved since sophomore year and, as seniors, were able to recognize what factors were most important to them in choosing higher education.

Junior Year

If you asked a group of graduating seniors what year of high school was the most difficult academically, I bet 99% of them would agree that junior year was indeed the most challenging. Not only are academics ramped up even more in all subjects, but also junior year is when the realization of getting accepted to a college hits home with most students. Up until this point, college hopes and dreams and eventual careers were all off in the distant future, somewhat intangible to the average, narcissistic teenager. But as junior year commences, the understanding that, "I need to really start seriously thinking about who I am, what I want to do, and what direction I want my life to take" materializes. The stress associated with juggling academics, sports, clubs, volunteering in the community and perhaps holding down a job is compounded by the addition of SAT preparation, résumé building, college research and campus visits. Add the constant chatter of peers discussing individual goals, college preferences and their most recent accomplishments and you have a very overwhelmed teenager on your hands.

REALITY CHECK

As a junior, my older daughter described the angst of applying to and thinking of attending college as a ticking alarm clock going off in her head. "You can't imagine how much I listen and think about this stuff (college chatter) at school. Everyone is always talking about what schools they are thinking about or have just visited. It is impossible not to compare yourself to everyone else!" This was the response I received when I first tried to broach the subject of college with Aly midway through her junior year. So, if you think your children are not thinking about or really doing anything to prepare for college, you may be wrong. While they may not be ready to talk about it or make any plans with you, rest assured, they are bombarded with information all day, every day during school hours.

There is not a definite date or time line that is right for all students to start the college search process in earnest, even during junior year. The timing has mostly to do with the personality of your child. Each of my three children handled the situation quite differently. My elder daughter started the college process with her fingers in her ears, basically kicking and screaming. She really did not have any idea what she wanted to do with her life so she was afraid to make any commitments. In February of her junior year, I took her on a Sunday afternoon just to visit, unofficially, some colleges near our home. It was an informal introduction to college life that at least started a dialogue between us. In April, we did the same type of visit but went a little farther—outside of our home state. Finally, in June before Aly's senior year, we went on our first official road trip. On the other side of the spectrum, my son, a rising sophomore, embraced the idea of college and was eager to join his sister on her college trip that June. He was open and not intimidated by the process at all. He had a more definitive future in mind so he viewed this as an opportunity to explore his options without any commitment. As a rising sophomore, my younger daughter, Victoria, went on the college road trip with her brother. Truth be told, she was much more interested in exploring the cities we were visiting rather than actually seeing the universities. Three children—each exactly two years and three months apart, raised in the very same home, in the same location, with the same parents—but each had a very different approach to the college search process.

As all parents really know, it is wise not to compare your children to each other or to their peers. Choosing a college is an individual process and each path is different and needs to be right for that child. Do not listen to other people's thoughts or ideas about college, *listen to your child.* Teenagers often speak but parents do not always hear what they are saying because it doesn't make sense to us. Listen carefully because they may only say something very important once. The good news to keep close to your heart during these trying times is that the teenagers in front of you today will, quite possibly, experience a complete transformation between junior and senior years. They will learn and grow as individuals and surprise you with their maturity by the time applications are submitted. If you are a doubting Thomas, have faith! As I talked about in Chapter #1, when my daughter Aly had less than four months left of her junior year, I thought for sure she would need to take a post graduate year because she was never going to be ready for college at the rate she was going. Little did I know at the time that not only would she figure things out, but she would apply to only one school early decision (ED) that November. In less than nine months after we finally started the process, Aly had come full circle recognizing the path she wanted to embark upon for her future. Did we do anything magical or hire any professionals to help? No. What we hope we did was listen to her and give her the tools she needed to visualize her own future in a way that built her confidence. Do we understand that this vision might change as she progresses through college? Yes. We only hope to have given her a solid foundation on which to build her future.

PARENT CHECK

At some point, before the end of your child's junior year, you may want to make an appointment with an advisor or the college counselor. This can be done with or without your student depending upon what you would like to accomplish but may be subject to the restrictions based upon the school's college counseling department. If your student has a separate high school advisor and high school college counselor, you should reach out to both of them. You should have a clear understanding of what you would like to accomplish at this meeting and discuss it with your student prior to the appointment. Transparency among students, parents and college advisors is absolutely necessary in order to build trust and accomplish the common goal.

VARIABLES FOR YOUR STUDENT TO CONSIDER DURING JUNIOR YEAR

1) Plan to **visit** some college campuses during the winter or spring vacations if your teenagers are ready.

2) Suggest high school **athletes** think about and decide whether or not they would like to play a sport competitively in college. If they are interested in playing Division I or II sports, they may have the opportunity to make some decisions about committing to a university during the first half of junior year. (See Chapter #7.)

3) Help your students evaluate when is the best time to take the **SAT/ACT** and determine when these tests will be offered. Explore whether they will take them more than once and whether they will want or need to take subject tests. (See Chapter #5.)

4) Encourage your students to develop **résumés** for themselves that include work, sports, community volunteering, clubs, etc. This will make it easier for them come application time if they already have this information updated.

5) Discuss with your students which teachers they will ask to write **recommendations** for their college applications as early as March or April. Make sure they ask the teachers before the end of the school year. Keep in mind that colleges are looking for teachers from junior and senior years that may also have had your students previously. (See Chapter #4.)

6) Suggest that your students think about an **essay topic** as early as May but definitely over the summer. Ideally, they should discuss this with an English teacher or guidance counselor before leaving for summer break. The essay should tell a college something about the students that cannot be gleaned from any other portion of the application. The essay provides a way for students to creatively express themselves. Suggest your students have a rough draft ready by the end of the summer so they can review it with a teacher, guidance counselor or trusted advisor when school starts in the fall. Every high school senior I've heard speak, at multiple public and private high schools, wished they had spent time on their essays the summer prior to starting senior year because it would have made their lives much less stressful. (See Chapter #4)

7) Remind your students to review and fill out as much as possible on the **Common Application** when it comes out in August. The more of it they complete before the start of school in September, the less stress they will experience when it comes time to actually submit the application. (See Chapter #4.)

See Appendix B for Junior Year Checklists.

Senior Year

Senior year is rife with excitement, anticipation, expectation, stress and waiting. As the summer months draw to a close, many students are coming into the fall with specific ideas about where they want to go to college. Others are still unsure. Again, this all depends upon the individual student. Often times, athletes will have committed to a school and are applying early decision. (ED is a binding commitment to a university.) These athletes have more than likely met with their coaches and have already discussed the merits of their applications. (Division III sports typically commit athletes in the fall of senior year. (See Chapter #7.) A smaller number of students will find a college that they are sure is the one and will plan on filing an application early decision as well.

REALITY CHECK

Trying to talk to students about college during this time will be challenging. Understand that they are constantly thinking about college, in fact, probably all day long. They are bombarded with information from peers, teachers, college counselors and even admissions officers who often visit local high schools. To determine whether or not your student is ready to listen or communicate about college is tricky at this time. This was very true for me with my daughter Victoria because whenever I tried to broach the subject of college with her, she would explode. In order to eliminate these episodes, we decided to only talk about college once a week. We both brought questions to our weekly meetings and updated each other on the status of past matters. Wednesday afternoons at four became our mutually agreed upon time. It worked extraordinarily well for us during the fall of her senior year because we both knew we could compile a list of questions that we could resolve on Wednesday afternoons. Victoria did not feel like I was harassing her and I did not feel like she was ignoring me or shirking her responsibilities.

During this time, students need to focus on narrowing their college choices. Nationally, a student applies to an average of four colleges, but it can easily go into double digits for some. Often times these school selections are characterized in three ways: likely, target and reach schools. Likely schools are those that students believe they can get into quite easily given their SAT scores, GPA, résumé, activities, etc. Target schools are those where a student has a fifty-fifty chance of acceptance. Reach schools are those students hope to gain acceptance to even though they may not possess every single factor the college is looking for. A student's college list should breakdown in thirds for each category. A guidance counselor at most high schools will talk to your student about these options, but a mantra for students to follow when narrowing their list and applying to colleges is for students to "like their likelies" and to identify their "favorite eight" colleges.

Making that final cut to the list of schools to apply to is difficult. When evaluating these choices, it is important for the students to consider the following variables:

1) Does the university **accept the Common Application or the Universal College Application?** If not, what does the application entail? (See Chapter #4)

2) If yes, does it require **supplemental essays?** If so, how many? If not, what else is required for the application? (See Chapter #4)

3) If your student is filing for a particular program such as Music or Architecture, are there any **additional supplements** required for that particular major? (See Chapter #4)

4) What type of **application review and processing** does the university offer? Early decision? Early action? Early action single choice? Early action priority? Regular decision? Rolling enrollment? (See Chapter #6)

5) What is the institution's policy on **recommendations**? How many do they require? Who do they suggest? (See Chapter #4)

6) Are **interviews** required, optional or nonexistent? If yes, with whom are they conducted? When are they conducted? Where are they conducted? (Alumni are often enlisted to interview potential candidates in their regions and report back to the university.) (See Chapter #4)

7) Is **financial aid** available? If yes, what forms are required? What are the due dates for the forms? When does a student receive the financial aid package that is associated with an acceptance? (See Chapter #8, Chapter #9 and Chapter #10)

8) Are there **scholarships** available? If yes, who is eligible? How do you apply? When are decisions made? (See Chapter #10)

9) What **standardized testing** does the university require? Do they accept both SAT scores and ACT scores or require any additional subject tests? (See Chapter #5)

10) What is the **cost associated** with filing the application? Do they have fee waivers? (See Chapter #6)

11) When does a student receive **notification** about decisions? Is it a rolling acceptance (acceptances disbursed over a period of time) or one definitive date (such as April 1)? Are students contacted via email, letter or both? (See Chapter #6)

See Appendix C for Senior Year Checklists.

PARENT CHECK

As you can see, there are so many nuances to the application process that it can be difficult to keep track of individual requirements. Answering all these questions up front before your student even decides to file an application can save time and anxiety in the coming months while also helping narrow the focus on college selections. I know one college that came off of Patrick's list just because its application required so many supplements.

Senior year is about the future, hopes and dreams. It is not a time for parents to impose their own expectations. This is definitely a gray area for all of us because it is difficult to know when to nudge your children along or when to step back and let them make their own decisions. Only you and your child can ford this stream, and you very well may find yourselves on opposing sides. If you are meeting resistance, it is important to ask yourself the question, "Why am I pushing so hard?" You must be able to answer this question honestly and without hesitation. Find non-confrontational ways to communicate your concerns and ideas. Explore new ways to inspire and motivate your students. By actively listening, you may discover important information you may have overlooked or hadn't considered. During this process, parents too, must be honest with themselves as well as their young, aspiring adults. This became very clear to both my husband and me as our son was looking at college. Always musically inclined, he wanted to pursue a very non-traditional path, at least in our family, by studying music. Since both my husband and I are first generation college graduates, we were worried that this path could lead to unemployment. Recognizing our concerns, Patrick came up with what we now call the back-up plan. He is studying music as he has always dreamed of doing but is also double majoring in Business Administration in order to insure there is some stability in his future. (To his surprise, Patrick has enjoyed learning about ways he can marry business and music in a career.) We definitely encourage and support all the goals and aspirations he has with his music, but we also sleep better at night with the knowledge that business is his back up. Communication and compromise have been essential in dealing with our own children as they entered adulthood.

college visits

STEP #1

Start with an unofficial visit to a local college.

STEP #2

Explore college webinars and information sessions offered on universities' websites before attending a local College Fair.

STEP #3

Have your students think about, talk about and research what would be an ideal university.

STEP #4

Book an official tour, information session and perhaps an interview on the university website. Use websites such as College Trips and Tips, www.collegetripsandtips.com, to help plan your visit.

STEP #5

Prepare questions about admissions, financial aid, student life, etc.

STEP #6

Find out the name of the Regional Coordinator at each institution who is responsible for your high school or geographic area.

STEP #7

Athletes and artists should contact the college coaches and the arts departments and set up a meeting or an appointment.

Start Locally

The quickest and easiest way to get the college process rolling is to start in your own back yard. If there is a university in your town, city or state, visit it with your students when it is convenient to do so. It does not matter if they would never consider applying to that particular college because what they really need to get is a feel for the size and location of the campus. Does it enroll 2,000 or 20,000 students? Is it in a city, suburban or rural location? Is there access to public transportation nearby? Is the campus open with facilities spilling over into the surrounding area or somewhat closed off to public access where the vast majority of the individuals on campus are students or faculty? Does your child like or dislike any of these scenarios?

Attend a Local College Fair

The independent, local, college fairs are usually held on a weekend afternoon in the spring and are promoted to high school juniors. I have found that they are well represented by an array of private colleges. The fair is set up in a booth format and an admissions staff member is there to answer any questions. This is a good opportunity for students to see the first face of a university as well as utilize their interpersonal skills in a public arena. (Often times, the regional coordinator for your geographic area is the admissions representative.) Although, many parents and students try to make this an opportunity for a personal encounter, the logistics and the number of attendees prevent this. The information disbursed is general although the admissions staff person will answer any questions. Finally, in addition to the traditional college fair, National Association for College Admission Counseling (NACAC) hosts a Performing & Visual Arts College Fair often held in many cities in the fall. For more information, go to www.nacacnet.org.

REALITY CHECK

It was the day of the college fair and Victoria was ambivalent about going. Truth be told, I really didn't want to venture out on a cold, wet April afternoon either, but I summoned my strength and forced us out the door. Victoria had not been very proactive about the college process thus far so I was hoping this would give her a little push. Once we were able to get off the mud soaked soccer fields being used as a parking lot and into the warm, dry gymnasium we were fine. The minute we walked in, we sensed excitement among these juniors. I noticed several engaged groups laughing and talking. I smiled thinking, "The reality and fear about college has not yet sunk into their psyches yet." This college fair was more like a social event, and the fact that so many of Victoria's friends were present made it easy for her to be drawn into the buzz. At the same time, it gave me the opportunity to look around and take in what was going on. What schools had the longest lines? Why was that college considered so hot right now? I have never heard of this one! What did Victoria's peers want in a college? Do they even know what they want? If you ask me if it was worth the trip, I would answer with a resounding yes because it was the first step Victoria took toward thinking more critically about college and the choices she would eventually have to make.

The Internet, university sponsored live chats and social media have given college-bound teenagers an alternative route to attending local college fairs. In an effort to cut back on travel costs and reach a broader audience, universities are utilizing the web to entice students to take a closer look at them. Students have the opportunity to speak to admissions staff people, current students and occasionally faculty from many universities while relaxing in the comfort of their own homes. Individual universities as well as companies like CollegeWeekLive, www.collegeweeklive.com, provide a forum for high school students and their parents to review the merits of a university while interacting with them in real time. These video chats, text chats and information sessions are free to students and their families, but independent companies do charge the university a yearly membership fee. Finally, students can also virtually tour any university in the country on the YouTube website, www.youtube.com.

Research

Have your students think about and research what would be the ideal university for them. This should start simply with not only a preferred field of study but also with geography – where they want to spend the next few years studying. This information will provide both of you with an understanding of how far they want to travel from home, their inclination for an urban versus a suburban setting or a preference for a student body of 4,000 or 40,000. It may be clear to you what is best for your child, but this is a developmental process that your students must go through in order to discover what they really want in a university and in life. This does not mean that you allow your child to go off on a tangent while you sit by without saying a word. In my opinion, it is the parent's job to guide their children through these decisions and to help them see what they can't see alone. I guarantee, where your students start is not where they will end up. A good place to start researching colleges is the U.S. Department of Education website, www.collegescorecard.ed.gov.

REALITY CHECK

After Aly and I had gone on that first infamous road trip where I learned never to ask, "Why crew?" again, we had a fair number of college visits under our belts. To move forward, we needed to narrow the parameters. One

thing I noticed was that Aly really did not like any of the universities we vis-
ited in cities, but she refused to let go of the idea of attending one. It wasn't
until we went back to her notebook and reviewed the list of pros and cons
that I was able to point this out. When she saw, in her own handwriting, that
she rated every urban college poorly, she finally got it and said, "Oh. I guess
I don't want to go to school in a big city." In my opinion, she liked the idea
of being in the city, but in her heart, she really was a small town college girl.

Official Tour, Information Session and Interview

After unofficially exploring some universities in your area and attending a local college fair, your students may start to get a better feel for the size and location they
would prefer in a university. The next step your students should take is to book an
official tour of a school that fits their current preferences. This would typically involve
a tour of the campus and an information session run by the Admissions Department.
The information session often communicates the philosophy and vision of the institution as well as the nuts and bolts including majors, class size, sports division, acceptance rate, the range of SAT scores and the GPAs of accepted students. Traditionally,
many universities offer morning and/or afternoon information sessions. It is best to
book this session in advance in order to ensure availability. To do so, go online to the
university's admissions website and view the calendar. Touring schedules can dramatically change throughout the year so be aware that the number of tours offered over a
spring break may not be the same as in January or February.

Many universities offer an interview as one component of the application process.
Someone from the admissions department, a student, or an alumna or alumnus of
the school may conduct these interviews in person, over the phone or via Skype. Find
out before you visit if any of these are an option. If available, your student should
decide whether or not it would be worth the time and effort. If the visit requires a
plane ticket or traveling a long distance, I would highly recommend signing up for the
interview in advance. It not only demonstrates that your student is a serious candidate
but also it may not be easy for you to return to the campus if interest rises. Recognize
that these days, universities do have many electronic and technological options for
interviews. Just make sure you know those options before you go.

REALITY CHECK

Each university adheres to its own schedule, but most offer information ses-
sions and tours throughout the early spring into the fall. During peak weeks
and the summer months, you may find both morning and afternoon sessions
available. This information can be important when scheduling a road trip. It

is very possible to schedule morning and afternoon information sessions and tours at two different universities when geography permits. I often did this with my college-bound teens and felt we got a good flavor of the campus by arriving early in the morning at the first and then staying late after the tour at the next one. We might eat breakfast, lunch or dinner in the cafeteria, at a local restaurant or just walk around to observe and explore. This time allowed us to take in the campus and view the surrounding neighborhoods or city. I felt this gave us a better sense of the pulse of the campus and student life.

Before You Go

1) **Look at the majors offered at the university.** Delve more deeply into the course offerings to see if that particular university offers what you are looking for. If your student, say, is interested in only Mathematics and a particular college does not have a strong Math department, you may want to consider whether this university would be the best fit.

2) **Find out if there are special tours for different major fields of study.** If your students are looking for a definitive major, such as Music or any STEM fields of study, have them contact that department to see if they have special tours or information sessions in order to find out more about how that program specifically works. Once your students sit in on an information session and decide that they would like to learn more, they should get the name of a student (usually your tour guide) with whom they can follow up with questions via Facebook or email.

3) **Find out if financial aid information sessions are offered.** Many schools do have financial aid forums, especially during the peak summer months. Attend at least one just to get your feet wet because, as you will discover, there are numerous aspects to this process. I have devoted three chapters in this book to financial aid.

4) **Print a campus map.** Your student should print a campus map before departing so you both will know where you are going. Find out the location of the Admissions Office and/ or your information session. Also, make sure at least one of you knows where to park. Having this information in hand prior to your visit will make your arrival much less stressful.

Once On Campus

1) **Drive around the campus and neighborhoods surrounding the college.** Both the parent and student should drive or walk around the entire campus as well as the surrounding neighborhoods while visiting a college in order to get a feel for the area. This should not only give both of you a geographic perspective but also provide you with a real feel for campus life and clarify some of the following questions: Is it an

open campus or closed? Is public transportation available? Are there any supermarkets, pharmacies, restaurants, employment or entertainment options close by?

2) **Record the colleges visit in a notebook.** I imagine that many young adults will fight their parents on this point, but it is extremely important for students to record information about each of the schools they visit. They should write down the pros and cons of each university and their impressions as soon as they leave the campus. If your students do not record their experiences right after visiting each university, I guarantee they will forget the details. Also, to enhance your college visit, connect with a current student on campus, pick up the college newspaper and visit the development office to find out more about internship opportunities as well as post graduate job placement. Once your child agrees to record their impressions, it is important that parents allow them to voice their opinions first. Parents' roles in this process should really be to ask pointed questions that will help their children objectively evaluate a college in order to see if it fits with their own interests and goals. (See Exhibit#1 for Visit Fact Sheet.)

3) **Ask Questions.** Parents and students should not be afraid to ask questions during an information session or while on a tour. The following is a list of some ideas that your student may want to entertain:

   a) **Admissions:** What is the timeline for the admission process? Does this institution support an early decision (ED) or early action (EA) admissions application? Are there multiple levels of the admissions decision-making phases (EDI, EDII, EA I EA II, EA single choice, regular decision)? What percentage of students do they take ED or EA? Are decisions communicated electronically or via the post office? Are all decisions communicated on a specific date or is it a rolling acceptance where students are notified throughout an extended period of time? (See Chapter #6)

   b) **Financial Aid:** What forms are required for financial aid? When are financial aid packages awarded and when do decisions need to be made? The majority of schools make their financial aid packages available before students have to make decisions as to whether or not they will attend a particular university, but there are some exceptions, especially for Early Decision applications. In the 60+ colleges I have personally toured, only one required a student to make a decision before receiving the financial aid information, but that institution did allow the student to opt out without a penalty if it was not financially feasible to attend. Students must check the policy of each university before applications are filed if financial aid awards are a deciding factor. (See Chapter #8, Chapter #9 & Chapter #10.)

   c) **Student Life:** Is the university a suitcase campus? What percentage of students lives on campus? Do many students leave campus to explore other parts of the city? Does the college have an Accepted Student's Day that allows a student to visit prior to accepting admission? It is quite surprising to many freshmen when they discover that the campus is empty on the weekends because many of their new friends live off-campus, go back home on Fridays or explore a nearby city instead. Knowing the answers to these questions will give your student a sense of how closely tied the student body is to university and campus life.

REALITY CHECK

Visiting college campuses with your children can be very exciting, nostalgic and fun, especially if you are prepared, but remember each child is differ-ent. I will be the first to admit that some of my teens were easier to enjoy on a road trip than others. In my experience, the ones who were less certain of their paths were more nervous (and maybe grumpier) at certain times.

Additionally, you and your student should recognize that college visits can be exhausting work. There is a lot of sitting, walking, driving, as well as frustration and unease from getting lost and eating on the run. (This may contribute to everyone's occasional flare-ups.) If you can tolerate all of this with your young adults and still focus, then bring along those toddler and elementary school siblings. If you are like me and know it could be a disaster, then divide and conquer. Leave those younger siblings at home with Mom, Dad, Grandma or a friend.

Contact the Regional Coordinator in the Admissions Department

Another important factor to consider when visiting a university involves making contact with the admissions department. Most universities' admissions officers are assigned to specific geographical areas. There will be at least one person in the admissions department who is responsible for your town and high school. This person, the Regional Coordinator, is usually the first one to read your student's college application and is often the individual responsible for presenting the application to the admissions board. It is the Regional Coordinator's job to get to know the schools in his or her area as well as the students who are applying to the university. I would highly recommend that your students seek out the Regional Coordinator and introduce themselves if there is any interest in that college. Meeting the Regional Coordinator may enable students to make a connection with one person who would be reviewing their applications if they decide to apply. Subsequently, if your students do wish to submit an application, they should contact the Regional Coordinator again to express interest or to clarify any questions. Many universities keep track of student visits and contact. This is called demonstrated interest. When students display enthusiasium and develop genuine rapport with the Regional Coordinator, they may be easier to remember when it is time to evaluate applications.

REALITY CHECK

Most Regional Coordinators travel to their geographical areas during the fall. They visit many high schools as well as hold forums in local venues. If students were not able to travel to the university or to meet the Regional Coordinator at a local fair or venue, they should secure the name and email address from the admissions office. Ascertaining the contact information of the Regional Coordinator will enable students to continue communication with him or her throughout the application process. In my experience, these coordinators are excellent at following up with students. They are almost super human in their ability to stay on top of the numerous emails they receive from potential candidates.

Athletes Visiting a College Campus

Sports in college can include a variety of options for the high school athlete. The opportunities to participate can be broken down into two levels. The top level includes sports that are subject to the rules and regulations of a collegiate governing body such as the National Collegiate Athletic Association (NCAA) or the Association of Intercollegiate Athletics (NAIA). This first level is differentiated by selective participation since only a discriminating group of athletes are chosen to compete. The second level primarily includes club and intramural sports' teams. As a rule, club teams tend to hold tryouts, be more structured and require the student to dedicate significant time to the program, while intramurals tend to be open to all students and faculty, are more flexible, and are usually for fun. If your students would like to play Division I, II or III sports, they will need to have contact with coaches at some point

Recruiting occurs in Division I, II and III institutions. Coaches look for players across the country to fill their rosters at camps, tournaments and platforms. They also talk to coaches from both high schools and club teams. Division I and II schools are typically looking at top athletes when they are rising juniors while Division III colleges do not firm up commitments with athletes until they are rising seniors. Although college athletic coaches are out there recruiting, there are over 480,000 athletes that are currently playing Division I, II and III sports in the NCAA. As a result, many athletes playing sports for Division II or III have not been recruited. So, it is important for students-athletes to reach out to the college coaches if they want to be a part of a college team. Subsequent contact should be made through emails, a meeting or a visit to the schools.

As your students plan athletic tours, they need to know as much about the team and the coach as possible. This involves not only looking at stats on a website, but also delving deeper into the team's philosophy. This could include asking questions of upperclassmen, fellow athletes, peers and coaches. Getting an objective read on the team may provide your student with insight or a perspective that he or she may have otherwise overlooked. (For more information on Athletics in College, see Chapter #7.)

Questions to ask on a Sports Visit

When your students plan their visits, they should have a list of questions prepared to ask during the meeting with the coach and use this opportunity to not only find out more about the coach, the team and the university but also about the nuts and bolts of the team organization. A few topics to consider are as follows:

1) The Coach: How does the coach operate the team? How long has the coach been at the university? Does the coach plan to stay?

2) Team Logistics: How cohesive is the team? What is the practice schedule? Are there double workout sessions in season? Out of season? Where are practices held? If it is off campus, how far away is the practice site? Is transportation provided for off campus practices? How long are the practices? What is the number of games, matches or regattas in a season? Are there any special requirements of team members such as living or dining arrangements?

3) Travel: How is travel handled for team members? How are academics handled if you have to travel during a testing period? Are there any holidays, spring breaks or summer sessions required for your sport? (I was surprised to learn that the crew coach administered final exams to her athletes in a hotel conference room, either before or after a race, when they occurred in season.)

4) Athletic Visit: Is an official athletic visit offered? (An Official Athletic Visit allows your student to visit the university to experience the team and university first hand.) Usually, a student would spend the night in a dorm with a team member and attend a practice, if applicable. NCAA rules strictly dictate the protocol for these overnight visits including testing the ability of an athlete.

5) Follow Up: Are there any current players that your student could be put in touch with to talk to via social media in order to get a better feel for the team or to follow up with more questions? What are the next steps in this process?

REALITY CHECK

Not all college coaches in all sports will meet with athletes individually. To gain enough information, have your child talk to high school coaches, club coaches, teammates, peers and college athletes in your sport to help get an understanding of how to approach this. Remember that playing sports in college needs to be a good fit for your student and for the team. If there are fundamental differences or conflicts between your student and the team or the coach's philosophy, then your student will probably not be happy and may end up quitting the team.

EXHIBIT 1   College Visit Fact Sheet

COLLEGE

NAME: _____

ADDRESS: _____

DEGREE OF DIFFICULTY: _____

SETTING: urban   suburban   rural   small town _____

SIZE OF STUDENT BODY: undergraduate _____
graduate _____

SIZE OF CAMPUS: _____

AVERAGE CLASS SIZE: _____

FACULTY TO STUDENT RATIO: _____

FIELD OF STUDY, MAJORS: _____

HOUSING: on campus   off campus _____

HOUSING GUARANTEED FOR 4 YEARS?   Yes   No

HOUSING STYLE: dorm   suite   private   semi-private

RATE DORMS 1–10: _____

FRESHMEN HOUSED TOGETHER: Yes   No

% OF STUDENTS WHO LIVE ON CAMPUS: _____

% OF STUDENTS WHO COMMUTE: _____

STUDENT LIFE

GREEK LIFE: Yes   No

ACCESS TO PUBLIC TRANSPORTATION: Yes   No

ACCESS TO RESTARAUNTS?   Yes   No

ACCESS TO EMPLOYMENT OPPORTUNITY: Yes   No

ACCESS TO A CITY: Yes   No

SUITCASE CAMPUS: Yes   No

SENSE OF COMMUNITY: Yes   No

ADMISSION REQUIREMENTS

APPLICATION: Common App   Universal

STANDARDIZED TESTING: _____

TEST OPTIONAL: Yes   No

BOTH SAT/ACT ACCEPTED: Yes   No

SUBJECT TEST REQUIRED: Yes   No
If yes, how many? _____

SUPPLEMENTS: Yes   No

APPLICATION SUBMISSION OPTIONS: _____

INTERVIEW: Yes   No

OF APPLICATIONS SUBMITTED: _____

% OF STUDENTS ADMITTED: _____

AVERAGE SAT/ ACT ACCEPTED STUDENTS: _____

AVERAGE GPA OF ACCEPTED STUDENTS: _____

AP CREDITS ACCEPTED: Yes   No

FINANCIAL AID

TOTAL COSTS (TUITION/ ROOM/BOARD/FEES): _____

FAFSA DEADLINE: _____

CSS PROFILE REQUIRED: Yes   No

CSS PROFILE DEADLINE: _____

INSTITUTION AID FORMS REQUIRED: Yes   No

COLLEGE FORM DEADLINE: _____

SCHOLARSHIPS AVAILABLE: Yes   No

TYPES OF SCHOLARSHIPS: _____

MERIT SCHOLARSHIPS: Yes   No

SCHOLARSHIP DEADLINE: _____

NEED BLIND OR NEED AWARE: _____

ACADEMICS

REQUIREMENTS: _____

OFFERINGS: _____

HONORS/SCHOLARS PROGRAMS AVAILABLE: Yes   No

HONORS/SCHOLARS APPLICATION DEADLINE: _____

STUDY ABROAD AVAILABLE?   Yes   No

INDEPENDENT STUDY AVAILABLE?   Yes   No

FRESHMAN SEMINAR REQUIRED?   Yes   No

COMPLIMENTARY TUTORING AVAILABLE?   Yes   No

CAREER CENTER

INTERNSHIP OPPORTUNITIES: Yes   No

RESEARCH OPPORTUNITIES: Yes   No

JOB PLACEMENT AFTER GRADUATION: Yes   No

BUSINESS OR INDUSTRIES CONNECTIONS?   Yes   No

% OF STUDENT PLACED? _____

SPORTS

DIVISION: I   II   III

CLUB SPORTS AVAILABLE?   Yes   No

TRY OUT REQUIRED?   Yes   No

INTRAMURAL SPORTS?   Yes   No

SPORTS INTEREST: _____

ARTS

SUPPLEMENTS REQUIRED: Yes   No

SUPPLEMENT DEADLINE: _____

AUDITION REQUIRED: Yes   No

AUDITION DEADLINE: _____

MISCELLANEOUS

IS THERE A BLUE LIGHT SECURITY SYSTEM?   Yes   No

IS THERE A QUIET ROOM IN THE LIBRARY?   Yes   No

NUMBER OF EATING OPTIONS ON CAMPUS: _____

EXHIBIT 1   College Visit Fact Sheet *(continued)*

PERSONAL ASSESSMENT

COLLEGE:

DATE OF VISIT:

ADMISSIONS OFFICER NAME:

EMAIL:

REGIONAL COORDINATOR NAME:

EMAIL:

TOUR GUIDE NAME:

EMAIL:

PROS

1)

2)

3)

4)

5)

6)

7)

8)

9)

10)

CONS

1)

2)

3)

4)

5)

6)

7)

8)

9)

10)

NOTES

OVERALL EVALUATION

CAN YOU PICTURE YOURSELF
ATTENDING THIS UNIVERSITY?   Yes   No

DOES YOUR GUT TELL YOU
THIS COULD BE THE RIGHT FIT?   Yes   No

WOULD I APPLY TO THIS UNIVERSITY?
                            Yes   Probably   Possibly   No

IF ACCEPTED, WOULD I ATTEND?
                            Yes   Probably   Possibly   No

OVERALL RATING ON A SCALE FROM 1–10:

VIBE OF CAMPUS: positive   negative   indifferent

DESCRIBE:

applying to college

STEP #1

Compare the Common Application and the Universal College Application.

STEP #2

Find out who will evaluate your students' applications.

STEP #3

Understand the components of the college application including student profile, standardized testing, high school transcript, essay, teacher recommendations, high school recommendation, university supplements, arts supplements, athletic supplements and the interview.

College Applications: The Common Application, the Universal College Application (UCA), and The Coalition for College

The Common Application, the Universal College Application and the Coalition for College are independent entities which provide a simplified application system for college admissions. Students complete these applications only once no matter how many schools they are applying to. Students may also have to complete application supplements for each university they apply to. The vast majority of students submit their college applications electronically.

The major differences between the established applications, Common Application and the UCA, are their philosophies, requirements and member schools. According to its website, "The Common Application is a not-for-profit membership organization committed to the pursuit of access, equity, and integrity in the college admissions process."[1] In addition to standard data and a personal statement or essay, it requires supplements and letters of recommendation. The Common Application has a membership of nearly 800 public and private universities. Alternatively, the UCA's intent is to make the college application process easier for students and reach a wide applicant pool. It also requires standard data and a personal statement but not supplements or letters of recommendation. It currently maintains a membership of 16 colleges. It is important to note that a university may still require recommendations or additional supplements in addition to the UCA. Before making the decision between the Common App and the Universal App, students should review the requirements of the colleges they want to apply to and, if possible, discuss it with a college counselor or an advisor.

The Coalition for Colleges, established in 2015 by a group of college administrators, is a newer entrant into the college application arena and is still tweaking its program. Its goal is to improve and enhance the college application and financial aid process for every student but especially supporting lower income, under-resourced and first generation teens. The Coalition believes all students, especially teens in under-resourced high schools, should have the opportunity to have additional guidance and encouragement to aid in the college planning process as well as boost their potential for success in college. It "is committed to making college a reality for all high school students through our set of free online college planning tools that helps students learn about, prepare for, and apply to college."[2] The Coalition for Colleges has 140 members for 2018–2019 and at least 10 more colleges committed to joining them in 2020–2021.

The Common Application

The Common Application membership association was established in 1975 by 15 private colleges that wished to provide a common, standardized first-year application form for use at any member institution. Today, the Common Application serves more than 800 colleges and universities across 20 countries.Each year, more than 1 million students apply to college through the Common Application. The Common Application is updated yearly and released in August for admission to a university the following year. It provides the basic framework needed to apply for admission to a college. It should be noted that most universities do charge a fee for each Common Application submitted. Clearly, this can become expensive when students go well beyond the average of four applications, but waivers are available.

The Common Application Requirements

a) **Profile**—Includes citizenship, gender and ethnicity.

b) **Family**—Includes siblings, parents' occupations and educational backgrounds.

c) **Education**—Includes course selection, advanced placement and honors classes, grade point average (GPA), class rank, official transcript, National Honor Society membership.

d) **Standardized Testing**—Scholastic Aptitude Test (SAT) scores and/or American College Testing scores (ACT); Subject Tests.

e) **Activities**—Includes sports, arts, clubs, student government, employment, volunteer activities.

f) **Writing**—Includes a personal statement or essay.

g) **Recommendations**—Includes at least one teacher recommendation the student has chosen as well as a recommendation from their high school college counselor.

h) **Arts Supplements**—Includes portfolios, recordings and video submissions.

i) **Individual University Supplements**—Often includes essays specific to each university.

The Common Application allows students to create accounts, add colleges to their lists, monitor the status of their applications and review deadlines of all the colleges they are applying to as well as upload and preview the applications before sending them. (This is done under the function of the Applicant Dashboard.) Although use of the Common Application is free online to applicants and recommendation providers, some colleges require a fee ranging from $25–$90 for a first year domestic application. For a complete list of the Common Application member colleges, go to www.commonapp.org/files/search/MemberList8_18.pdf.

REALITY CHECK

Each of my three children submitted the Common Application electronically for all the colleges they applied to. All three felt that it was relatively easy to use, tracked the status of their applications well and made sense given the requirements for the universities to which they applied.

Universal College Application (UCA)

Much like the Common Application, the UCA enables students to apply to multiple colleges using a single application. While it may seem there are fewer requirements on the UCA, many colleges will ask for more from students. It is wise to check each university's individual requirements before filling out any application. For a complete list of Universal College Application member colleges, go to www.universalcollegeapp.com/colleges.

UCA Requirements

a) **First Year Application**—Personal information, citizenship, ethnicity, family information, personal statement.

b) **Instructor Recommendation**—Applicant/instructor information, background on student-teacher relationship, applicant rating in academic/character/personality traits, evaluation of academic and personal traits of the applicant.

c) **School Report**—Academic information, current courses, advanced placement courses or International Baccalaureate exams taken, standardized test information, extracurricular and volunteer information, employment information, personal statement given by guidance counselor.

d) **First Marking Period Report/Mid-grade Report/Final Report**—Applicant/counselor information, academic information including course names and levels (AP and honors), GPA, school profile, background and applicant ratings, evaluation of applicant, official transcript—all submitted by the high school.

e) **Arts Supplement**—Applicant personal information, resume, letter of recommendation from an instructor, visual or audio submission in area of artistic talent via the Internet link or CD/DVD.

f) **Athletic Supplement**—Applicant information, area of athletic interest, coach's name, specific awards, records, times.

g) **Early Decision Agreement**—Applicant information signed by the student, a parent and guidance counselor.

The Coalition for Colleges

The Coalition for College believes all students, especially teens in under-served areas and high schools, should have the opportunity to pursue a college education. The Coalition offers students, as early as ninth grade, the opportunity to use MyCoalition, a college planning and application forum, in order to help them learn about, prepare for, and apply to the 140 member colleges who use this application. The Coalition's application shares many similarities with the Common APP and the UCA, but the requirements for the application will vary by university. Students should review the application requirements for any colleges they would like to apply to and, if possible, discuss this with a counselor or mentor. It should be noted that most universities do charge a fee for submitting a college application but fee waivers are available for eligible students through The Coalition. For a complete list of The Coalition for College member schools, go to www.coalitionforcollegeaccess.org/alert.html.

The Coalition Application Components

a) **Student Profile**—Includes student's name, date of birth, email, sex, gender (optional), social security number, Armed Forces status, expected college enrollment date, financial aid applicant, and Community Based Organization (CBO) participant.

b) **Family Information**—Includes family size, education, siblings, residency and guardian information if applicable.

c) **Writing**—Includes an essay where a student may choose from 4–5 prompts with one option being a topic of the student's choice.

d) **High School Information Section**—Collects information about your high school and grade level. It also includes:

   1) **Recommendations**—Includes at least one teacher recommendation students have chosen as well as a recommendation from their high school.

   2) **Transcripts**—Includes a school report and high school transcripts.

e) **Standardized Testing***—Scholastic Aptitude Test (SAT) and or American Testing scores (ACT); Subject Test (if applicable).

f) **Individual University Supplements***—Often includes additional essays specific to each individual university.

g) **Supplements***—Optional, additional material submitted as part of the application that can include projects, photos, videos, artwork, awards, essays, letters, service, research or capstone projects.

*Individual Universities that are members of the Coalition for College may have different or optional requirements for students filing their college applications. To verify requirements, please check with each college of interest.

Who Evaluates the Application?

If you have ever watched the movie *Admission* with Tina Fey, you have seen the exaggerated, comedic view of the college admissions process, but behind every joke, there are hidden truths. For the most part, one person, the Regional Coordinator for your school or demographic area, is in charge of learning about your student and following his or her application through the process. The Regional Coordinator is often the person who pitches your student's application to the admissions committee when it comes time for decision making. Typically, at least two admissions staff members will have read your student's application prior to it being reviewed by the committee for admission.

REALITY CHECK

I feel it is vital for students to make a connection with their Regional Coordinators. Obviously, each university has certain criteria that they are looking to meet as well as a desire to accept a diverse group of students, but they also want to admit students who want to attend their university and who bring something new, fresh, interesting or dynamic to the culture. Whether it is a passion for Civil War History or an interest in baking that makes someone a better candidate for a particular university, it is the connection with the coordinator that could tip the balance in your student's favor. Remember, these admissions officers meet and read thousands of applications every year. Steve Thomas, former Director of Admission Colby College 1998-2014, said it best at a forum I attended in 2014. His words were, "Make me remember you!" Have your students make every effort to show the Regional Coordinators who they are and why they would be exceptional choices for those colleges they really want to attend.

Components of a College Application

These include: a student profile, standardized testing scores, high school transcripts, teacher recommendations, a high school recommendation and individual university supplements. (Additional supplements may be accepted or required for the arts or a sport. Personal recommendations from a mentor/teacher/coach in your specialty may be submitted as well.) The vast majority of this information is forwarded electronically to each individual college but hard copies are available as well.

a) **Student Profile**

The profile section of the application often includes personal information about students, their activities, work history, ethnicity, citizenship and family. Family information includes details about siblings' ages and education as well as parents' backgrounds, education, occupations and financial status.

REALITY CHECK

The students quite easily fill out the profile portion of the application with minimal input from their parents. In our house, these questions were asked and answered informally during family dinners.

b) **Standardized Testing**

The majority of colleges require students to take the Scholastic Aptitude Test (SAT) or the American College Test (ACT). In the past, the general public had a perception that the SAT was the superior test but that image has changed. In 2012, more students took the ACT than the SAT. Not only do all U.S. colleges now accept the ACT, but they also do not prefer one test over the other.

In the past, the SATs and ACTs were two very different and separate tests that measure similar but very distinct constructs. The ACT measures achievement related more to high school curricula, while the SAT was geared toward evaluating general verbal and quantitative reasoning. The debate over whether these tests truly indicate a student's ability to succeed in college continues. This ongoing discussion has led the SAT to redesign their test effective March 2016. Also, it has led some universities to become test optional, allowing applicants to decide whether or not to submit SAT or ACT scores.

REALITY CHECK

Since standardized testing is such a high profile component of the college application, I have devoted a separate chapter to it. For a complete guide to standardized testing, including the SAT, ACT, SAT Subject Tests and Advanced Placement Tests, please refer to Chapter #5.

c) **High School Transcript**

An official high school transcript will be sent directly to the colleges students are applying to by the college counselors and the guidance office. One of the first pieces of a transcript that a college looks at is the students' grade point averages or GPA scores. GPA calculations vary by school based upon curriculum and course offerings. Many high schools and most colleges look to report GPAs on the standard scale of 4.0. Some high schools use grade distribution charts instead of calculating GPAs. These high schools prefer to rely on the content of their curriculum as a reference point for colleges. Both of these methods are usually familiar to admissions staff members who are able to interpret the meaning behind the numbers.

As I mentioned in the second chapter, a student usually has to have been in the same high school for two years before a GPA is calculated. So, the first time students see their GPAs on a report card is often at the end of their sophomore years. In addition to a standard scale 4.0 GPA, there is also a weighted GPA, which takes into account advanced placement (AP) and honors classes. It is based upon the idea that these classes are tougher and should be weighted to reflect the difficulty associated with the course work. Weighted GPA scales vary by school but can often go as high as a 5.0. AP and honors classes should raise a student's Cumulative GPA when calculated as advanced classes. To calculate a Standard 4.0 scale or weighted GPA, go to www.wikihow.com/Convert-a-Percentage-into-a-4.0-Grade-Point-Average. (Note: While wikihow may not be the most academic website, it does provides a clear and simple explanation of GPA calculations.)

REALITY CHECK

In addition to GPAs, many universities also look at students' course selections, their class ranking and the overall direction their grades have taken. Most colleges have Regional Coordinators whose job it is to be very familiar with the curriculum and course offerings at the schools in their areas. That coordinator is usually one of two individuals who will review your student's application and he or she will look to see if an applicant has chosen an easy or a more advanced course load. These more difficult courses prove that the students who manage them successfully in high school will be able to succeed in college. If there are some grades that are not quite what students had hoped for early on in their high school careers, don't panic. Most universities are really looking for grades to have an upward trajectory to reaffirm that students have grown and matured and were able to handle more strenuous courses as they progressed through high school. Conversely, an unexplainable downward spiral with grades during junior or senior year is a red flag for colleges and may very well indicate that the student is not ready to manage a rigorous college curriculum at this point.

d) **Essay**

The essay portion of the college application is the one section over which the student has complete control. The essay is often open-ended in its subject matter but does have a specific length requirement by the majority of universities. Typically, it has a minimum of 250 words and a maximum of 650. This is the one time throughout the grueling application process that your children can truly express themselves. From Cornell to Tulane and University of Vermont to Wesleyan, the message is the same. The essay portion of the college application should be a personal statement where students should SPEAK UP. The essay enables colleges to learn so much more about the true identity of students.

Once students have written their rough drafts, they should find one or two people who will read them and give constructive feedback on the content. (An English teacher or advisor at school is a good choice.) Remember, the essays should be evaluated on technique, not topic or tone. Students should expect to have to rewrite their essays, often several times, before submitting them.

For the 2019–2020 Common Application, there are 7 essay prompts available for students to choose from with the last one being an essay on a topic of the student's choice. For a list of the current Common Application essay prompts, Google search "Common App Essay prompts" or go to www.commonapp.org/whats-appening/application-updates/2019-2020-common-application-essay-prompts.

Essay Specifications for Coalition for College

Although the Coalition application does not designate a specific length for the essay, they do suggest students aim for 500–550 words but strongly advise students look at individual universities' essay requirements because it may vary.

For 2019–2020 Coalition for College essay, there are 5 prompts available for students to choose from with the last being an essay on a topic of the student's choice. For a list of the current Coalition for College essay prompts, Google search "Coalition for College essay prompts" or go to www.coalitionforcollegeaccess.org/essays.html.

REALITY CHECK

The following comments are a collection of DO's and DON'Ts regarding the essay I have gathered from high school advisors and college admissions officers over the last six years.

DO

> *Be yourself.*
>
> *Be genuine.*
>
> *Be honest.*
>
> *Be boastful, but not arrogant.*
>
> *Assume the reader knows nothing about you. Step back, introduce yourself.*
>
> *Get your personality across.*
>
> *Find the tone you want to communicate.*
>
> *Keep it personal.*
>
> *Find your voice.*
>
> *Make it about you.*
>
> *Speak to who you are.*
>
> *Show who you are.*
>
> *Take control.*
>
> *Recognize that you have the power.*
>
> *Make a connection with the admissions officer.*
>
> *Make the admissions officer remember you.*

DON'T

> *Be shy.*
>
> *Try to out think the admissions' staff.*
>
> *Write about what you think admissions would like to hear.*
>
> *Write about something that is already on your resume.*
>
> *Write a funny story if you are not funny.*
>
> *Write about someone else who is amazing.*
>
> *Let anyone tell you what subject to write about.*
>
> *Let anyone change the tone of your essay.*

Clearly, the essay must be well written and grammatically correct, but the subject matter and how it is delivered is what is most important. Steve Thomas, former Director of Admission at Colby College for 16 years, said, "The essay is about the glue and the pearls. The glue is what you write about and the pearls are what we can learn about you that we cannot learn anywhere else. When you are finished, circle the pearls in your essay. (See if that is what you want to communicate.) I need to remember you."

e) **Teacher Recommendations**

Most universities require two teacher recommendations. These teachers should have had the students they are writing recommendations for as juniors or seniors. If certain teachers have had students in their classes more than once during high school, they would be excellent choices because they can speak about how those students have changed and grown over time. Each teacher students ask to write recommendations should know them in different capacities. For example, if a student is passionate about science, it would be better to have one teacher recommendation come from the Biology or Chemistry teacher and the other from an English, History or French instructor. Again, try to make sure that each teacher your student asks will write a positive recommendation.

REALITY CHECK

I once heard an admissions officer say that teachers' recommendations are hugely important to the college application process because teachers are brutally honest. It is very important that students ask teachers who genuinely like them. Teachers have been known to write poor recommendations about students.

f) **High School Recommendations**

Usually, your student's college advisor or guidance counselor is the person who will write the high school recommendation. The purpose of this recommendation is to further allow admissions officers to get to know students. In order to write better recommendations, some high school counselors ask parents to fill out questionnaires to help with the details regarding the students' lives. They are often looking for specific antidotes in order to tell a story about the student. Parents, take the time to fill these questionnaires out thoughtfully. Much of the feedback you provide will be included in the recommendations.

REALITY CHECK

If there are any gaps, unusual changes or bumps in the road (such as an illness or transfer of schools) during your student's high school years, the best place to address them is here in the high school recommendation part. In my opinion, it is better to explain a situation than to leave a college admissions officer guessing as to why something happened. There is no need for speculation if you and your student are preemptive and clarify circumstances that may appear questionable on the surface. Talk to your student's college counselor about this if you have any concerns.

g) **University Supplements**

Both the Universal College Application and the Common Application require personal statements or essays that allow students to make an impression on the admissions board. In addition, many universities across the country require additional specific information such as additional essays or a section of short answer questions. The most common questions range from, "Why do you want to attend College X?" and "What experiences have attracted you to a specific field of study at College Y?" to more specific personal questions such as, "What books or publications have you read recently?" and "What films, concerts or exhibits have you viewed and enjoyed in the past year?"

REALITY CHECK

Each university is looking for something different, but what they all have in common is that they would like the answers to these questions to truly reflect the persona of the applicants. As a result, students should respond honestly and creatively. If taking risks, responding unexpectedly or being playful is part of who a student is, go for it. Reading into whether or not the question calls for a serious or silly response is appropriate but students who attempt to tailor their answers according to what they think the admissions department is looking for, will learn that this is not a good idea. Students should be themselves but their smarter, stronger, most confident selves—the genuine people they want the universities to see. The truth is students need to attend colleges that embrace them, not someone they are trying to be.

h) **Arts Supplements**

Students who have special talents in music, dance, theater or visual arts often submit supplementary arts materials for evaluation by the admissions department. Each university has its own recommendations, requirements and deadlines depending upon the artistic medium. Information about students' arts backgrounds and samples of their artistic work may be submitted online through the Common Application if the selected university uses the Slide Room portal.

Since May 2013, the Arts Supplement (of the Common Application) has been replaced by **Slideroom.com**, which is used by approximately 170 colleges. All other schools may host their own art forms. "The end goal of SlideRoom is to create an easy submission process for applicants as well as an efficient viewing environment for admissions staff. Slideroom is completely web-based so there is nothing to download, install, or maintain."[3] For more information on Slide Room and a list of participating colleges, go to www.slideroom.com/commonapp/.

As noted, not all universities that are members of the Common Application utilize Slide Room, but instead provide their own external provisions for submitting arts supplements. Since the list of universities utilizing Slideroom.com through the Common Application is constantly changing, it is best for your student to follow up directly with the admissions office or the university website to confirm how art supplements are submitted. Additionally, it is important to remember that even those institutions who do utilize Slide Room may have multiple requirements that the Common Application does not track. Ultimately, the onus is on your student to confirm that each facet of the arts supplement has indeed been completed and submitted.

Even though the Common Application does enable many students and affiliated universities to transfer arts supplements electronically, the Universal College Application still offers the option for students to manually submit CDs/DVDs or to provide a link to view a student's work. According to the website, "Applicants with a significant interest or talent in art and/or music and wish to provide samples, may do so as part of the Arts Supplement."[4] Students may "provide a CD or DVD of no more than 5–10 minutes, which demonstrates your artistic ability. (Please send copies and be sure to clearly mark your name on the submission. Colleges may not return supplementary materials.)"[5] Also, it allows a student to provide a link for online work. For more information about the Universal Application Arts Supplement, go to www.universalcollegeapp.com/resources.

REALITY CHECK

Advancements in technology should help alleviate and hopefully eliminate the loss of arts supplements that happened a lot when snail mail and even YouTube were used in the college admissions process. My own experience with my son shows that students must follow up until the very end to ensure that their arts supplements are seen by the admissions staff, not just the Music or Theatre departments. As a senior in high school, Patrick knew he wanted to pursue music in college. As part of his admissions application, he wrote, arranged and performed two original songs and sang a cover in a studio which he rented and paid for himself. He forwarded the CD to all to the designated admissions/music departments of all his early action choices and followed up to confirm its receipt. As he waited for a decision, he felt confident and proud of the work he had done. When he received an email on Saturday, December 15, from a top choice school that said he had been deferred, he was crushed. My husband and I were dumbfounded given his academic standing as well as the artistic work he had done completely independently, all the while rowing for a nationally-ranked crew team. We devised a plan which involved Patrick calling his Regional Coordinator directly that Monday morning. To his surprise, she answered the phone. As they spoke, Patrick learned that his arts supplement never reached the admissions office as his application was being reviewed. Somewhere along the line, there was a disconnect between the Music department and Admissions. In hindsight, I made a mistake. I do remember him asking me specifically if he should follow up again with that college after he had a confirmation from the music department about the receipt of his CD. Since it was after the November 15 EA deadline, I advised him not to do so because I thought it was inappropriate. I was wrong! He should have followed up again to ensure that his Regional Coordinator in the admissions department knew to look for his music supplement.

i) **Athletic Supplements**

For many years, athletes have provided coaches with footage that displays their talents and superior performance. Today, college coaches are exposed to athletes at tournaments, showcases, summer camps and other platforms that are specifically designed for this. Additionally, college coaches are in contact with well-known clubs and high school teams who generate quality athletes. As a result, by the time athletes are submitting their college applications, they have more than likely spoken to or had some contact with college coaches. Even though the need for athletic supplements has diminished over time the Common Application has recently enabled universities to choose whether or not they would like athletic supplements added as an option in SlideRoom. "If you decided to submit a supplement (Athletic, arts, etc,) SlideRoom will charge you a $10 fee for each submission. These supplements are not required. We encourage you to present yourself the best way you can within the format of The Common Application."[6] The Universal College Application has an athletic supplement form that is used by its members. "Applicants with areas of athletic interest may provide more detail such as positions played, letters earned, and specific accomplishments as part of the Athletic Supplement."[7] The Universal Application does not mention submitting a DVD or electronically uploading footage to be reviewed.

REALITY CHECK

Athletics in college is big business. If you are looking to play a sport in college and you are not an athletic prodigy being recruited by all the DI top universities, then you have to do some work to attract the attention of the coaches. Don't think, "They can come to me," or "I'm not good enough." Be proactive. Contact the coaches directly through email or a telephone call and introduce yourself. If you are planning to visit the school, make an appointment to meet with the coach. You may be surprised at how many coaches, even from the most prestigious schools, are willing to talk to or meet with an unknown athlete.

In the summer when Aly was a rising senior, she had hopes of rowing in college. Even though she had only been rowing for a year, she and her high school coach were convinced she could have a rowing career in college. Regardless of my reservations, I encouraged her to contact all the rowing coaches at the schools we were visiting that summer. To my surprise, all of them were willing to meet with us. Granted Aly's high school crew team was the Massachusetts State Champions for several years and frequently had boats competing at nationals, but she had just finished her novice year as a rower. The real surprise came about half way through our college visits when we toured a very beautiful, prestigious college that had a women's crew team. After our tour and information session, we drove to the boathouse to meet with the head coach. He was a kind Southern gentleman who could tell we were very new to this process. In that hour-long meeting, he graciously took the time to educate us on crew and gave us several suggestions as to how we should go about finding the right college and crew team for Aly. It wasn't until we had spent about 45 minutes with him that I realized he was the coach of the team that had just won the NCAA Championship a month earlier! Initially, I was horrified that I had, basically, forced Aly to set up this meeting and we had taken up so much of his time, but he then spoke of his philosophy about finding athletes in places that many coaches don't even consider looking. Clearly, this was working for him!

j)   **Interview**

Many universities offer interviews by someone from the admissions department, current students or alumni, which can be held in person, over the phone or via Skype. Interviews not only provide an opportunity for your student to learn more about a particular university, but also allow the university to learn more about your student's strengths. Taking the time to interview often shows the university a higher level of interest on the part of the candidate. Since universities want to admit good students who are highly interested in attending their institution, an interview can be a means to personally convey students' interest as well as their personalities, reasons for wanting to attend that university and any connections to the school.

Passion is a characteristic many admission administrators look for in future candidates. Whether it is for fishing, fashion, history or athletics, the subject of the student's passion does not matter. In the eyes of many college administrators (and future employers) students with passion have the drive and desire that often leads to success.

Students should find out before they visit a college if any interviews are an option. If they are, students should decide whether or not this would be worth the time and effort given their interest level in the school. If your visit requires a plane ticket or traveling a long distance, I would highly recommend signing up for the interview because it definitely shows a high level of interest and it may not be easy (and could be expensive) to return if your teen's interest grows. Recognize that universities have many options with technology now to interview potential candidates, so make sure you explore those options before you go. Note: the typical dress code for most college interviews is casual but clean. Although there are few shirts and ties visible on male candidates, especially during the summer months, you may spot some females in summer dresses staying cool in the heat.

REALITY CHECK

You would think by the time I was sending my third child off to college, I would have learned my lesson about interviews, but, sadly, I had not. When Victoria and I planned a college road trip, there were a couple of schools she was very interested in. As I began to plot out how we could get to all the schools we needed to, I discovered that one school on her list offered Saturday tours and information sessions but did not hold interviews over the weekend. (I did not know at the time that an interview was looked upon very favorably at this particular university and could potentially make a significant difference when it came time for admissions.) In order to visit as many schools as we could on our college tour, we decided to forgo the interview and visit that particular school on a Saturday. That was a mistake. As Victoria's knowledge and self awareness grew, this particular university became a top choice for her. When we met with her college counselor that fall, she suggested, if feasible, that Victoria go back there for an interview because it could make all the difference in her application. As a result, we had to rework high school and employment schedules and pay to get her back for an interview. Not only was this difficult and costly, but I also noticed that Victoria had become quite nervous about this interview. My normally confident, talkative, cheerful teen seemed a little less engaging and self-assured when she walked into that interview. If I could have turned back the clock, I would have made sure we visited that school on a day when interviews were being offered.

████████████████████████████████

Talking Points and Interview Questions

- Tell me about yourself.
- What do you think about your high school?
- What would you change?
- What is the most recent book you read and why?
- What is your favorite subject and why?
- If you could go back in time, where would you go and who would you want to be?
- What are your interests (and passions) outside of school?
- What are your goals for your future?
- Why University XYZ?
- What do you think you might like to study in college?
- How would you be involved on our campus?
- What other colleges are you considering?
- Do you have questions?

The Coalition for Colleges Distinction

The Coalition for Colleges' mission is to make college more accessible for all students but it is focused on making a difference for underserviced students from lower income families, under-resourced high schools and first generation college teens. In order to accomplish this goal, the Coalition has not only developed an accessible, college application but some unique features to better prepare students. These additional features include the Locker, the Collaborative Space and the College Counselor found in the "On-line Tool Kit." "The Coalition's online toolkit, MyCoalition, is designed to engage students in the college application process early and easily. It is comprised of a convenient digital storage Locker, interactive Collaboration Space, and easy-to-use application which is accepted at all (140) member schools."[8] For a complete list of The Coalition for College member colleges, go to www.coalitionforcollegeaccess.org/alert.html.

A Locker

The Coalition Locker is a private, online, free, unlimited storage space within My Coalition. This is where students can collect, store, organize and share important materials and documents that they may use as part of their college application. Students are encouraged, as early as ninth grade, to start saving important materials such as projects, photos, videos, artwork, awards, essays, letters, service, research or capstone projects, and any other materials of significance. Materials are securely stored in the cloud for several years and can be easily submitted as part of the student's application to Coalition colleges.

B Collaborative Space

The Collaborative Space is a virtual space where students can share and discuss their work with their family, mentors, guidance counselors, advisors, coaches or any trusted adult they deem appropriate. Students can contact any of these individuals from the Collaborative Space through email and share material that they would like feedback. These "trusted advisors" can then provide comments for the students on the work in a side bar but they cannot change the students' work. This space is often used with students and their supporters to review essays, college lists, or applications.

C Coalition Counselor

The Coalition Counselor is a listing of resources a student can reference to find advice on topics including financial aid, standardized tests and college essays. This includes up to date articles, checklists and printable expert advice.

To learn more about the Coalition for College and open an account to begin utilizing the "On-line Tool Kit", Google search "Coalition for College", or go to http://www.coalitionforcollegeaccess.org/ .

CHAPTER 5

standardized testing

Recognize that the SAT and the ACT are accepted at all four year U.S. colleges.

STEP #2

Know that the format of the SAT changed in the spring of 2016.

STEP #3

Identify the components of the SAT.

STEP #4

Understand how the SAT scores are calculated.

STEP #5

Identify components of the ACT.

STEP #6

Understand how the ACT scores are calculated.

STEP #7

Understand the implications of test optional schools.

STEP #8

Consider having your students take both the SAT and the ACT.

STEP #9

Help your students determine which test is best for them to focus on and perhaps retake.

STEP #10

Determine if your student needs to take the SAT Subject Tests.

STEP #11

Understand the implications of Advanced Placement (AP) testing for college.

STEP #12

Evaluate the options for SAT or ACT test preparation.

Overview

Standardized tests are "less important than you think but more important than we'll tell you."

—Steven Thomas,
Former Director of Admissions,
Colby College

As I mentioned earlier in the book, it has been debated whether standardized testing really measures students' capabilities or indicates success in college. Because of that, some universities have decided to become test optional, allowing the students to decide whether or not to forward their SAT or ACT scores. Even though admissions officers may down play the significance of these test scores, the fact remains that the vast majority of universities still require standardized testing. At one college forum I attended, Mr. Thomas, who is quoted above, got quite a laugh with his words because he actually said what all of us in the audience had been thinking! I appreciated his honesty.

As I mentioned in Chapter #4, in the past, the general public had a perception that the SAT was superior to the ACT, but that image has changed. Twelve states require and pay for all public high school juniors to take the ACT. In 2012, the ACT actually pulled ahead of the SAT for the first time: "1,666,017 students took the ACT while 1,664,479 took the SAT."[1] "All four year U.S. Colleges now accept the ACT" and and "most colleges do not prefer one test over the other."[2] As a result, many students are taking both the SAT and the ACT.

In the past, the SATs and the ACTs were two very different and separate tests that measured similar but distinct constructs. The ACT has always been known for measuring achievement related more to high school curricula, while the SAT was geared toward evaluating general verbal and quantitative reasoning. This all changed in March of 2016 when the SAT redesigned their test. The objective of the redesigned SAT was to provide a more comprehensive picture of a student's readiness for college. To accomplish this, the SAT completely altered their format and subsequently tweaked some of the aspects of the test. Since the redesigned test was implemented, test scores seem to be 50–80 points higher for current students than scores from students in the past.

In general, students taking the SAT have more time with each question while the ACT are about speed. If your students feel more comfortable taking one test over another, let them do so but if they are open to the idea, consider having them take both tests to see if one is better suited than the other.

REALITY CHECK

A common practice found in the college application process is called super scoring. In the past, many universities would super score the SAT and ACT results. What that means is that a college will cherry pick your student's highest scores per subject. Some universities even super-duper score these tests. This means that the university will take your student's highest SAT and ACT score for each subject and use the highest combination of scores to evaluate your student's application. Both of these strategies help bolster your student's application, and they also make the universities appear to accept students with higher scores.

A. Scholastic Aptitude Test—SAT

The Scholastic Aptitude Test (SAT) is a standardized test accepted for college admissions in the United States. Although colleges and universities utilize the test as a component in evaluating a student's application, they are not the ones who actually create the test. The test is written by the Educational Testing Service (ETS), a nonprofit company in the business of creating tests for school admissions and other diverse professional groups. The SAT is designed to assist in determining one's academic readiness for college, but it has often been criticized for not measuring the skills students really need to be successful in college. To combat this perception, the SAT ushered in a new redesigned test in March 2016. "The SAT is (now) focused on the skills and knowledge at the heart of education: It measures what you learn in high school (and) what you need to succeed in college and career training."[3]

The 2019–2020 SAT will run 3 hours with 50 minutes for an optional essay. "Occasionally, the SAT will pretest new test questions to determine whether they should be included in a future SAT test form. These questions may appear in any of the test sections and testing time will be extended by 20 minutes so students have time to answer them."[4] At this time, the components of the test are as follows:

- Reading Test (65 minutes) Writing and Language (35 minutes)
- Math (80 minutes)
- Essay (optional 50 minutes)

The College Board and Khan Academy have joined together to provide 20 hours of free practice testing that can be tailored to students based upon SAT or PSAT/NMSQT scores. There are "free and affordable resources to help you (students) do your (their) best."[5] They are available to all students, anytime and anywhere. For more information, visit www.collegereadiness.collegeboard.org/sample-questions.

Scoring on the SAT

Current scoring on the SAT shares similarities to the past but delves deeper with additional reports. Familiar components of SAT scoring are as follows:

> **Total Score (1):** Math and Evidence Based Reading and Writing combined equal one score maximized at 1600.

> **Section Scoring (2 total):** Math score and Evidence Based Reading and Writing scored independently ranging from 200–800.

> **Essay (Optional) Scoring (3 total):** Scale ranging from 2–8 with results reported separately for Reading, Writing and Analysis.

The additional scoring analysis since Spring 2016 includes:

> **Test scores (3 total):** Reading, Writing and Language, and Math scores represent performance across subsections of the exam have scores that range from 10 to 40.

> **Cross-test scores (2 total):** A score for Analysis in History/Social Studies and a score for Analysis in Science will both fall between 10 and 40. These cross-test scores represent performance on specific questions in these sections.

> **Subscores (7 total):** Four subscores for skill areas in Reading and Writing and three for skill areas in Math will range between 1 and 15.

Note: Little is known about how, or even if, college admissions officers will use the test and cross-test scores. It is possible that specialized college programs will be more interested in some test scores than others. Time (and college admissions officers) will tell but it is important to remember that these scores do appear on your teen's SAT Score Reports which are sent to all admission departments to which your student applies.

An official report will be sent to students and their high school college counselors within three weeks. Colleges will receive scores no later than 10 days after that. Students who registered for the SAT online, creating a College Board account, can review their scores on their phone or a computer as soon as scores are released. Those who register by mail will not have a College Board account and may only receive their results in the mail.

Most students take the SATs more than once. Opinion varies on how many times it is appropriate and productive to take the tests. I would suggest that this is an individual decision based upon the personality of your students. If the SAT fosters anxiety, I would not suggest your student take the test numerous times. If your student can handle it and believes that repeating the test will improve scores, then go for it. It is important to note that some top tier colleges require students to send all of their scores from all of the SAT exams. Research exactly what the policy for SAT scoring is at the colleges your students are interested in before deciding how many times they should take the test. It is important to confirm whether or not the university super scores your student's tests.

The SATs are typically offered seven times during the school year. In the past, they have been slotted for August, October, November, December, March, May and June. It is important to note that many of those test dates work well for seniors applying to college regular decision. For any senior who is interested in applying to a college early decision or early action, the October test date is probably the best, and may be the only option. For more information about specific dates and registering for the SAT, go to www.collegeboard.org.

B. American College Test—ACT

Created by ACT Inc., the American College Test is an entrance exam acccepted by colleges and universities to make admissions decisions. The purpose is to provide American colleges with a common archetype to compare all applicants. In addition to college testing, ACT Inc. provides other assessment, research, information and program management services for education and workforce development. Clients include elementary and secondary schools, colleges, professional associations, businesses and government agencies on a national and international level. The organization states that the "ACT products and services have one purpose—helping people achieve education and workplace success."[6]

Overall, the ACT test for college applicants takes three hours and 30 minutes to complete and is broken down into five sections. These sections include:

- **English**—"One 45-minute section, 75 multiple choice questions measuring your understanding of English, production of writing and knowledge of language skills.
- **Math**—One 60-minute section, 60 multiple choice questions measuring mathematical skills students have typically acquired in courses up to the beginning of grade 12.
- **Reading**—One 35-minute section, 40 multiple choice questions measuring reading comprehension commonly encountered in first-year of college curricula.
- **Science**—One 35-minute section, 40 multiple choice questions measuring the interpretation, analysis, evaluation, reasoning and problem-solving skills required in biology, chemistry, Earth/space sciences and physics.
- **Writing**—One 40-minute optional writing section measures writing skills taught in high school English classes and in entry-level college composition courses."[7]

Scoring on the ACT

Each subject area—English, Math, Reading, Science and Writing—is scored independently. Scores are calculated by the number of questions answered correctly. There is no penalty for questions answered incorrectly and subsequently no negative repercussions for taking an educated guess. The raw score, or the number of correct answers, is converted to an ACT scaled score that ranges from 1 to 36. The four scores are then combined to generate a fifth called the composite score. The composite score is the average of the four test scores, rounded to the nearest whole number. "The average ACT composite score for 2018 was 20.0. To get a good ACT score for 2018, you'll typically need to aim for at least the 75th percentile, or 24–25 on each section."[8]

The releases of ACT scores vary over a range of weeks based upon the test date, but are updated weekly. Although multiple choice scores are released first, all scores, including the ACT with Writing, should be available within eight weeks of a students test date. Once scores have been finalized, ACT, Inc. will release official reports to the student, the teen's high school and colleges requested. Students can access these scores through their online ACT web account which they created when they registered for the test.

The ACT is offered nationally, seven times a year, during the months of September, October, December, February, April, June and July. Again, many of those later dates are options for seniors who plan to apply to college regular decision. For seniors who are interested in applying to a college early decision or early action, the October test date is the latest they can take the test. For more information about specific dates and registering for the ACT, go to www.actstudent.org.

Test Optional Universities

In recent years, there has been an increasing trend among some universities that allows applicants to choose whether or not they want to submit their SAT/ACT scores. The rationale for this has sprung from the idea that standardized tests do not portray an accurate picture of a student's aptitude or likelihood to be successful in a college environment. These universities are de-emphasizing the importance of the standardized test in the college admissions process. Among the universities that support this approach are New York University, Wake Forest (North Carolina), American (Washington DC) and Bethesda University of California. For a complete listing of universities that are test optional visit www.fairtest.org/university/optional.

Some institutions make it very clear that the SAT or the ACT is not necessary or important in the application process. Some test optional schools indicate that the absence of standardized test scores won't hurt students but the inclusion of strong test results will definitely help. In my opinion, there are some unwritten rules at certain prestigious universities about whether or not submitting test scores will impact acceptances. Students should discuss this issue with their college counselor and their Regional Coordinator from the university in question.

REALITY CHECK

When Aly narrowed her college search to one school, she was relieved that it was test optional because she had not done as well as she had hoped on her last SAT primarily due to illness. When it came time to apply early decision (ED) that fall, she was in a quandary about submitting her scores. She had actually taken the test again and was proud of having improved her scores quite a bit. Still, she couldn't decide whether to submit the SAT results or not. "Would it look like I am hiding something if I don't, or will it hurt my application because they may not be good enough?" This dilemma consumed her until I suggested she talk to her guidance counselor. Mrs. G's knowledge of that college's admissions history as well as Aly's credentials helped her decide that she should submit her scores.

C. SAT Subject Tests

The SAT subject test is an hour-long exam that enables students to demonstrate proficiency in a specific subject. They are the only national admissions tests that allow students to choose which test to take in order to best illustrate their academic accomplishments and interests.

There are 20 SAT subject tests in five areas: English, History, Language, Mathematics and Science. Some universities require applicants to take one or more SAT subject tests. These tests evaluate students' knowledge of that particular subject based upon content. The SAT subject tests are often considered more akin to classroom related work.

Subject tests are offered six times per year in August, October, November, December, May and June. Although most tests are available on each date, your student should review the schedule, confirm the test is offered, and see when it makes sense to take that particular test. For example, most juniors take the U.S. History SAT subject test in May just as they are finishing their year-long course on U. S. History. Similarly, if students take Chemistry as sophomores, they should consider taking the SAT Chemistry subject test in May or June of that year but recognize that independent study may be necessary since most high school curricula do not cover all topics on subject tests.

Raw scores for these tests are calculated based upon the number of questions answered correctly, while a fraction of a point is subtracted for wrong answers. (No points are deducted for unanswered questions.) That raw score is then converted to the College Board 200–800 point scale. The mean subject test scores vary from test to test because different groups of students take different tests, but the average scores for college-bound seniors in 2018 ranged from a 607 in English Literature to a 760 in Chinese with Listening. For more information on the SAT Subject Tests, go to www.sat.collegeboard.org.

The following is a list of the SAT subject tests:

Literature	U.S. History
World History	Math Level I
Math Level II	Biology/EM
Chemistry	Physics
French	French with Listening
German	German with Listening
Spanish	Spanish with Listening
Modern Hebrew	Italian
Latin	Chinese with Listening
Japanese with Listening	Korean with Listening

REALITY CHECK

SAT subject tests are required by many elite schools as part of the admissions application. For example, a few of the Colleges at Cornell University require students to submit scores from one or two subject tests. If a university requires subject tests and your students did not take them, they will not be able to submit an application. For a list of colleges that require, recommend or consider SAT Subject Tests in Admissions, go to collegereadiness.collegeboard.org/sat-subject-tests/about/institutions-using.

In theory, the SAT subject tests allow students to differentiate themselves in the college admissions process by identifying strengths and aptitude. It is often regarded as another piece of information that provides a more complete picture of a student's academic capacity and pursuits. Additionally, some universities use SAT subject tests to place students into the appropriate course level. Based on their performance on a subject test, student can potentially fulfill a college requirement.

D. Advanced Placement (AP) Testing

Advanced Placement classes are offered in many high schools across the country. A student typically needs to be recommended by a teacher or department in order to be placed in an AP course. AP courses are considered more prestigious by many universities because the workload is more challenging. In many instances, high school students are doing college-level work. As a result, the student is working toward not only gaining confidence and experience but, potentially, college credit.

The AP courses offered at individual high schools vary, but the AP test offerings are very specific. There are a total of 38 AP tests available in the U.S. Although each test has its own individual requirements, they all have the following factors in common:

1) **AP Tests are approximately three hours long.**

2) **The first section of the exam** consists of multiple-choice questions where the student chooses one of four or five potential options for each question.

3) **The second part of the exam** usually consists of open-ended questions that require students to generate their own responses. Depending on the exam, the responses could be essays, solutions to problems or, in some instances, spoken responses. In most cases, students will be writing their responses in an exam booklet.

4) **The exam score is based upon the number of questions the student answers correctly.**

5) **Students are not penalized for incorrect answers or for omitting a question.**

All AP tests take place during a two-week period in early May. All students around the world take the same AP tests on the same day, typically at their own high schools. If a student is ill or has an excusable absence, there is a make-up test week in late May. The final score for each test is reported on a scale of one to five and illustrates how well a student has mastered the content of the AP course. Many universities waive a college requirement or give credit if a student scores a four or five on an AP exam. AP results are available in July and are released to students, their high school college counselors and designated colleges. Students who created a College Board account before July will be able to review their own results online. For more information on Advancement Placement exams, please go to apstudent.collegeboard.org.

The following is a summary of the Advanced Placement exams for 2019:

1) **AP CAPSTONE:** AP Research, AP Seminar.

2) **ARTS:** AP Art History, AP Music Theory, AP Studio Art 2-D Design, AP Studio Art 3-D Design, AP Studio Art Drawing.

3) **ENGLISH:** AP English Language and Composition, AP English Literature and Composition.

4) **HISTORY AND SOCIAL SCIENCE:** AP Comparative Government and Politics, AP European History, AP Human Geography, AP Macroeconomics, AP Microeconomics, AP Psychology, AP United States Government and Politics, AP States History, AP World History .

5) **MATH AND COMPUTER SCIENCE—STEM:** AP Calculus AB, AP Calculus BC, AP Computer Science A, AP Computer Science Principles, AP Statistics.

6) **SCIENCES—STEM:** AP Biology, AP Chemistry, AP Environmental Science, AP Physics C: Electricity and Magnetism, AP Physics C: Mechanics, AP Physics 1, AP Physics 2.

7) **WORLD LANGUAGES AND CULTURE:** AP Chinese Language and Culture, AP French language and Culture, AP German Language and Culture, AP Italian Language and Culture, AP Japanese Language and Culture, AP Latin, AP Spanish Language and Culture, AP Spanish Literature and Culture.

REALITY CHECK

Some of the AP Tests are notorious for being extraordinarily difficult. It came as a surprise to me that Music Theory fell into this challenging category. My son, Patrick, sang, played the piano, wrote music and studied Music Theory from the time he was five. When he signed up to take the AP Music Theory test, he held out little hope of scoring a four or five which surprised me. As it played out, he scored a three, a solid effort but not good enough to be waived out of his Introduction to Music Theory class in college. The story does not end there, though. Flash forward to Patrick's first day of classes at Tulane University that fall. He walked into his Intro to Music Theory class and written on the board was an inverted chord. After the class settled down, the professor asked, "Who can tell me what this means?" Patrick and a few other students raised their hands. The professor responded: "You shouldn't be in this class. This is what we will finish covering at the end of the semester. You need to go to the registrar and enroll in the next level of Music Theory."

Tutoring and Prep Classes for SATs and ACTs

Many friends and family members have asked for my thoughts on prepping students for standardized tests. With my own children, there were mixed results with group sessions and one-on-one tutoring which were run by a national chain and local experts. So, what have I learned from these encounters? Before you even start with a tutor, have your students take both the SAT and the ACT to see if one test plays more to their strengths. If they score measurably higher on one test over another, continue to focus on prepping for that one. If there is no clear advantage, allow your students to choose which test they are most comfortable taking. Once you understand where your students need to focus and would like to pursue some preparation for standardized testing, I strongly suggest the following:

1)   **Get a recommendation.** Employ a tutor or group that has been referred from a trusted source who is willing to share honest, real information about test scores.

2)   **Get the name of a specific person.** If an agency is recommended, get the name of a tutor with whom your contact has had success.

3)   **Meet the tutor.** Meet the person who will be tutoring your student. Ask some questions about the curriculum. Decide for yourself if you think he or she is worth the investment.

4)   **Identify a philosophy.** Find out the philosophy of the company or tutor you plan to employ. You may be surprised at the diverse approaches. (Content versus strategies) I have discovered that teaching strategies for these standardized tests is the best preparation.

5) **Make sure your student feels comfortable** with the teaching style and personality of the tutor. If your student doesn't like or doesn't get a good feeling from the tutor or program, do not use them.

6) **Don't settle.** If you or your student is unsure of a program or a tutor, do not proceed. I guarantee it will be a waste of time and money.

7) **Plan ahead.** Figure out when is the best time for your student to prep for the SAT or ACT. Keep in mind that the fall of senior year is still a good time to take standardized tests, even for early decision applications. Your student can still prep during the summer before senior year and take the ACT in July or the SAT in August.

REALITY CHECK

The majority of students consistently score higher on the practice SAT/ACT tests than they do on the official tests. Many attribute this to the level of difficulty of the exams or nerves, but there are some hidden factors that may impact your students' scores come test day, even if they have prepared well. The following are some facts to consider before your student signs up for any standardized test:

1) **Where is your student taking the test?**
Students should take the standardized tests in an environment where they are comfortable. For some students, that means being in familiar surroundings with peers, but for others, it means being anonymous. Talk to your students and find out where they would be most comfortable.

2) **Is your student anxious?**
If students are anxious, they may be afraid that this is the one and only shot at doing well and getting into college. A parent should reiterate that they can always take the test again and that the vast majority of colleges super score standardized tests. As I mentioned at the beginning of this chapter, this means that a college will cherry pick your student's highest scores per subject regardless of when they took the test.

3) **Is your student confident or presumptuous?**
A confident student will most likely be calm and focused when taking the test, but a presumptuous student may take things for granted and make mistakes. There is a fine line to walk between the two. Victoria decided to take her SATs again after having improved her score significantly when she prepped with a tutor. The night before the test, she had a friend over to watch a movie and stayed up pretty late. The result—there was an overall drop in her test scores. When we spoke about it afterwards, she admitted that she had grown a little over confident given her success on the previous round.

4) Is your student feeling ill in any way?

If your students have the sniffles or are ill in any way, chances are good they are not going to perform well even after a lot of prep work. Reassure them that it will be fine and let them decide whether to take the test that day. When Aly took her SAT in the spring of her junior year, she had a terrible cold and felt miserable. Even though she had prepped independently and with a tutor, she did not do as well as she had hoped.

5) Does your student own it?

Students who are going through the motions, doing the practice tests and seeing a tutor but not necessarily internalizing the need to do their best, will not perform to their highest potentials. When all three of my children took the SAT for the last time, it was a decision they each made independently, without input or influence from me or their Dad. In the fall of her senior year, Aly decided she wanted to take the SAT again because she had been ill when she took it in the spring. She worked independently to prepare and seemed to be more serious this time. The result was the kind of scores she had hoped to get the first time. When it came time for Patrick to take the SATs, he had prepped primarily on his own but did join a group Math session. He did as he expected but thought he could do better on the Math portion. He decided to take the SATs one more time but only really focus on prepping for the Math. The result was that Patrick increased his Math score by 60 points. When Victoria realized she had misplayed her last SAT test, she decided to refocus and take it one last time in December of her senior year. Confident but cautious, she was able to bring her overall score up 90 points. Though each scenario was different, each child took control of their situations and decided they needed to do this for themselves. Although, it is easy to see in hindsight, I would be willing to bet that you have a sense of what type of effort your child is putting forth. In my opinion, when all three of my children decided to own their SAT scores, and I mean take full responsibility for realizing their importance and the value of preparing, they did their best.

Hindsight

If I could go back in time and do one thing that would have helped my three children prepare for their college SATs in a non-structured way, it would have been to incorporate more vocabulary into our everyday lives. Vocabulary is pivotal in the reading, writing and English section of all standardized tests. The obvious solution is for them to read more, but realistically, by the time teens come home from high school after sports or a job, eat dinner, do homework and take a shower, there is little time for you to even have a conversation with them, never mind encourage reading for fun.

I can tell you that now that I am here again with my high school sophomore, Reece, I realize just how difficult this is to do in reality! Not only does it take monumental effort on my part as a Mom, but when you couple that with a less than willing student who doesn't quite see the benefit of prepping vocabulary when he finally has some down time, it is close to impossible to do. Nevertheless, we will forge ahead doing the best we can.

submitting the application

STEP #1

Determine your students' readiness to select colleges to apply to by reviewing their list of universities. This list should be balanced, with a third of the schools falling into each category of "likely," "target" and "reach."

STEP #2

Determine your students' interest in or commitment to one school.

STEP #3

Review application submission options. This means identifying the timing and commitment required. (See Reference Guide below.)

STEP #4

Identify what application submission options are available for each college of interest making note of deadlines and binding agreements.

STEP #5

Develop a plan for all application submissions.

STEP #6

Identify dates your students will be notified of admissions' decisions.

STEP #7

Identify when a commitment to the university is required, noting that most agreements require a deposit by May 1 in order to secure a space for your students.

STEP #8

Review application submission options again. A quick reference guide is provided below.

Quick Reference Guide for College Application Submissions

- **RD—Regular Decision**—non-binding application to multiple schools filed January 1–February 1; notified by April 1.

- **ED—Early Decision**—binding application for only one school filed by November 15; notified by December 15.

- **EDI—Early Decision I**—binding application for only one school filed by November 15; notified by December 15.

- **ED II—Early Decision II**—binding application for only one school filed by January 1; notified by February 15.

- **EA—Early Action**—non-binding application to one school or several filed by November 15; notified by December 15.

- **EA—Early Action Single Choice**—non-binding application to only one school filed by November 15; notified by December 15.

- **EA—Early Action Restrictive**—non-binding application to one school filed by November 15; notified by December 15.

- **Rolling Admission**—non-binding application to one or several schools filed over an extended time frame; no standardized notification dates.

- **Open Enrollment/Open Admission**—no agreements, deadlines or notifications; enrollment is available for any high school graduate.

Overview

This chapter describes the timing and parameters associated with filing a college application. As you can tell from the numerous options, there are many variables as to when and how students file their applications. Even though the national estimate suggests that a student applies for admission to an average of four universities, application submissions for one person can easily go into the double digits. As a result, it is imperative that students check with each individual university and their high school college counselors to confirm deadlines and requirements.

Choosing which application to file depends on students' readiness to commit to one university or not. Application choices have been referred to as alphabet soup because of the acronyms associated with them. The following is an in-depth summary of the college application deadline terminology and the implications:

Regular Decision (RD)

1) Regular decision applications are normally filed between January 1 and February 1.

2) Regular decision applications are non-binding agreements that allow students to apply to multiple colleges without committing to one.

3) Regular decision notifications are usually sent out anytime between mid-March and April 1.

4) Regular decision candidates typically must commit to a university by May 1.

REALITY CHECK

Applying RD allows students to continue to explore which college they would really like to go to while still entertaining some options. Regular decision is the right choice for students who may be too young or need to gain more self-confidence before committing to a university. It is also the last chance for students to apply to any college for admission the following September. Alternatively, RD is often used as a strategy for students to apply to some reach schools without a binding commitment. From the university's perspective, it is their last chance to admit the best candidates into the freshman class, but it can be difficult to project their yield given the number of applications most students submit. As a result, some universities cast a wide net with acceptances and waiting lists in order ensure a quality freshman class.

The total number of schools a student applies to for college admission can range dramatically. Aly, Patrick and Victoria applied to one, seven and five schools respectively, but in my immediate circle of friends and family, some teens applied to upwards of 13–15 universities. Most of these applications will fall into the RD pool because students recognize that they want options, and it is their last chance to be considered. Since there is a cost and some work associated with every application, the question students should ask themselves if they are applying RD to more than 10 universities is, "Would I even consider attending College XYZ if I am admitted?" If the answer is definitely, "No," why bother?

Early Decision (ED)

1) An early decision application allows students to learn if they have been accepted early in their senior years.

2) ED is a binding agreement wherein if students are accepted, they must attend the following year.

3) Early decision candidates can only file one application.

4) An early decision agreement must be signed by the student, parent and school counselor.

5) ED applications are typically filed starting in October with a final deadline by November 15.

6) ED responses are normally released by mid- to late December.

7) ED applicants may have a higher acceptance rates than regular decision candidates at some universities because an ED application demonstrates to the university a more committed student, and the university can count on that student attending. For this same reason, universities may accept ED candidates with lower GPA or SAT scores than the norm if the student has demonstrated a high level of interest in the college or has a unique skill or aptitude to offer. Students should talk to their high school advisors to discuss a university's philosophy on ED.

Early Decision I versus Early Decision II

1) The primary difference between early decision I and early decision II is timing.

2) Universities that offer both EDI and EDII have two separate deadlines for application submission and the decision notification.

3) EDI submission deadlines typically fall around November with decision notifications released by mid-December. EDII submissions are often due around January 1 with decision notifications released by mid-February.

4) EDI and EDII applications are binding agreements between the student, the parent, the school counselor and the university. EDI and EDII applications commit that student to that one particular college if accepted.

5) A student may only file one EDI application at a time.

6) If students do not gain admittance to an ED or EDI school prior to the due date of an EDII application, they may file an EDII application at that point. Under no circumstance can students file an EDII application if they are still waiting for a college to respond to an ED or EDI application.

7) The early decision agreement that is required of all EDI and EDII applicants must be signed by the student, parent and school counselor.

REALITY CHECK

Students' decisions to apply EDI or EDII are usually the same as those for students who apply ED. These students know which college they want to go to and are willing to forgo acceptance to any other institution if they get in. In some instances, they are also motivated by more relaxed admissions criteria. EDII gives students who may have been denied entrance to a top choice school the opportunity to apply early to another university. Again, in the EDII pool, the university is guaranteed that the students they select will attend.

A good friend submitted an ED application to a university that he considered a reach. The application was due on November 15. He heard by December 15 that he did not gain admission. As he evaluated his next steps, he realized that his second choice offered EDII. Again, this school was a bit of a reach as well, but he decided to take the chance. He submitted his EDII application before the January 1 due date and received an email notification on February 15 that he had been accepted.

It is important for students considering early decision to understand their reasons for doing so because not only is it a binding contract, but also it is a decision made very early in the process. The 17- or 18-year old standing before you in November will quite possibly feel differently come May.

A final consideration to make regarding ED applications involves financial implications. If the financial aid package offered by the college does not sufficiently cover the costs for students to attend, they or their parents may need to nullify their binding contract. Universities MAY release students from binding contracts due to insufficient financial aid packages, but these families may have to prove extreme financial hardship in order to be released. Since policies vary by institution, all students applying ED should check with the individual universities before submitting their applications.

Early Action (EA)

1) Early action applications are typically filed by mid-November and decisions are usually received by mid- to late December.

2) EA applications are non-binding agreements that allow students to apply to multiple colleges without committing to one.

3) EA decisions must be made by May 1.

4) A student who applies EA may also apply to any other public or private university early decision, regular decision or rolling decision. (See exceptions below.)

5) Early action offers students the most flexibility if they are prepared to attend college but would like to continue to explore what university will be the best fit.

6) Early action acceptance rates can be higher than RD based upon the institution's agenda in a given year.

7) If applicants are deferred during the EA period, their applications will be reviewed again and considered with the regular decision applicant pool.

REALITY CHECK

Decisions to apply early action are often based upon the fact that students like many schools and are not yet ready to commit to one. EA gives students definitive answers about some options by December 15. Knowing they have been accepted to a school they feel is a good option tremendously decreases students' stress levels. (Many students apply to some safety schools EA just for the reassurance that they have been accepted somewhere and are going to college!) With EA, universities are obviously not guaranteed that the students they select will attend, but it allows them to offer spots to qualified students before they have applied to other universities. Since EA does hinder a university's ability to predict student yield for a given year, schools offer variations of early action.

Early Action (EA) Exceptions

A. EARLY ACTION SINGLE CHOICE

An early action single choice application is another form of early action. Many aspects of the application are identical but there are several factors that are clearly distinct. The following summarizes the policies and distinctions of an EA single choice application at most universities:

1) EA single choice is also filed by mid-November

2) EA single choice decisions are usually received by mid- to late December.

3) EA single choice is a non-binding application but it **limits a student's application** to only one university.

4) EA single choice decisions must be made by May 1.

5) A student who applies EA single choice can apply to other universities regular decision or rolling decision as long as those decisions are non-binding.

6) EA single choice most often **precludes a student from applying early decision** to any other private institution.

7) EA single choice applications often have higher acceptance rates than EA applications because colleges know the applicants are seriously interested in attending. When students narrow their options by applying EA single choice, institutions look a bit more closely at their applications.

B. EARLY ACTION (EA) RESTRICTIVE

EA restrictive is another version of EA but it has its own unique implications depending upon the university. If students plan to apply EA restrictive, it is extremely important they follow the college's guidelines. In general, the following is a summary of the unique parameters associated with EA restrictive:

1) A student applying to a binding early decision (ED) program may not apply early action restrictive.

2) A student applying to a binding early decision II program may apply early action restrictive if the due date for submission of the former is after the EA restrictive decision has been released.

There are differences among universities as to whether or not students can apply to other universities early action if they are applying to a college early action restrictive. For example, Harvard and Stanford's policies do not allow students applying EA restrictive to apply to any private college EA but does allow them to apply EA to any public college/university or to foreign universities with a non-binding admissions process.

REALITY CHECK

Most universities utilize only one variation of early action, but since rules do vary by institution, students should verify procedures at their colleges of interest. Students decide to apply early action single choice or early action restrictive if the school is very high on their list of options but they are not quite ready to commit to it. These students are willing to forgo all the other EA opportunities. Universities have instituted EA single choice and EA restrictive because it distinguishes a student's commitment to their institution providing a more predictable student yield.

Rolling Admissions

1) Rolling admissions typically gives a student a larger window of time to apply to a university.

2) Rolling admissions often opens in the early fall and may continue throughout the summer.

3) Students are often notified of a decision within a few weeks of applying.

4) Most universities accept students who meet their criteria as long as there is space in the class.

5) Rolling admissions may not have any specific application deadlines, but there are deadlines for scholarships and financial aid. An early application can improve a student's chance of acceptance as well as the availability of housing, scholarships and financial aid awards.

6) Few selective colleges use rolling admissions deadlines.

REALITY CHECK

Students decide to apply rolling admissions because they can apply without a commitment and they often find out quickly if they are accepted. It is interesting to note that not all rolling admissions schools notify students right away. A family friend submitted an application in the fall to a noteworthy university that had rolling admissions but did not receive any notification until the spring. Even though he was accepted, the constant anticipation and delayed notification actually played a role in deterring him from considering this college.

Open Enrollment/Open Admissions

An institution has open enrollment or open admissions if its application process includes the following:

1) The college requires only a high school diploma or general equivalency diploma (GED) in order to admit students.

2) The institution does not evaluate applications based upon a student's grade point average.

3) The university does not usually require either the SAT or ACT for admission.

REALITY CHECK

Students decide to apply to colleges with open enrollment or open admissions because it is easy, the requirements for admission are minimal, it is usually less expensive, they can choose to attend part or full time and they can start at the beginning of any semester. The goal of most institutions with open enrollment is to make education accessible.

Variations on Application Submissions by University

As you can tell, there are numerous timing options for students to file their college application. Again, it is always wise to check with each individual university and your high school college counselor before proceeding because there are many rules and exceptions. The following are a few individual practices that existed and I personally came across in the last six years when going through the college application process with my own family and friends.

A. Early Evaluation Option (Wellesley College)

Wellesley College is a suburban, female, liberal arts school with a student body of approximately 2,500 located in Wellesley, Massachusetts. Princeton Review rates it as highly selective. The application process at Wellesley College does include early decision and regular decision with an added feature called early evaluation. The early evaluation plan provides students with an indication of their chances for admission at the end of February. Candidates who apply Regular Decision with Early Evaluation option are told if their chances for admission are likely, possible or unlikely.

B. Priority Application (University of Maryland)

The priority application at the University of Maryland is promoted by the university as a way for students to receive the best consideration for admission as well as for merit-based scholarships and invitations to special programs. Although there are similarities to EA, its application deadlines and notifications are unique.

C. VIP Applications/Fast Applications (Fast Apps)

VIP applications/Fast apps are the same as Presidential Select, Select Scholar and Priority. The VIP/Fast applications typically offer a quick, simplified application process for a limited time for select students. Over the years, there has been some controversy surrounding these applications with respect to their rationale and true purpose. Critics in higher education believe they are a marketing tool for colleges to increase their applicant pool quickly and raise the SAT scores of that pool. A good rule of thumb to follow when filing applications is: "Do not apply to a school just because it appears to like you. Only apply to a school that would fit you personally and academically."

D. Individual College Filing
(University of California at Berkeley)

UC Berkeley does not use the Common Application or Universal College Application but provides its own. The UC Berkeley application is available August 1 and currently has a December 15 deadline for freshman applications. It includes essays, a personal statement and SAT or ACT scores, but it sets slightly different criteria for applicants who are California residents versus out-of-state residents.

Meeting Application Deadlines

As with all components of the college application, submission and notification deadlines vary slightly by institution. Since the majority of college applications are submitted electronically, students need to be aware of any time variations that exist. For example if you live in Chicago (CST) and are submitting an application regular decision (RD) to Duke University in North Carolina (EST) that is due on January 1, does your application need to be filed by 11:59 Eastern Standard time or can it be submitted by 11:59 Central Standard Time? Although it may seem inconceivable to a parent that a college application would be submitted minutes before the deadline, you would be surprised at how many college-bound seniors press the send button just before midnight. According to the Common Application website, "To meet an application deadline, you must submit your application materials by 11:59 PM on the deadline date posted on your Dashboard. The end of the deadline date is in your local time zone, not the college's time zone. Keep in mind, all timestamps are recorded in EST (US Eastern Standard Time). It is always better to submit well before 11:59 pm to avoid last minute issues with your computer or internet access that might cause you to miss the deadline![1] It is worth noting that all of the components of the application should be submitted or postmarked by the deadline date. This includes any recommendations and arts or athletic supplements (CDs or DVDs) that cannot be submitted electronically.

It is relevant to point out that it is the students' responsibility to make sure that all the components of their applications have been received by the institution. Just because they know that all the pertinent documents were sent from their high schools, it does not guarantee that they have reached their final destination and are available for review. Students may view their applications online to check the status. If sufficient time has passed and an application is listed as incomplete, the student should check which records are missing. Following up to make sure all the pieces of the application are intact will not only eliminate last minute stress but also ensure that it is reviewed in the best light. If pieces are missing for unforeseeable reasons, your student should contact the high school college counselor immediately to resolve these issues.

REALITY CHECK

To eliminate any further anxiety, I cannot stress how important it is to make sure your students have checked and confirmed the status of their applications. Remember my story about my son, Patrick, in Chapter #4? Because I counseled him not to follow up on his application components after the deadline for decisions was made, he was deferred from one of his top choices. Luckily, he figured out the problem, was given another chance and was ultimately accepted. Still, had we checked and double-checked, a whole lot of useless stress and worry could have been averted. Advise your student to follow up on each and every facet of the application! Do not be afraid to break what you or your student think may be protocol.

I would also advise your students to follow up on their applications more than a couple of hours before the deadline. On November 15, 2014, Victoria was checking to make sure all of the pieces of her ED application had been submitted. Her heart skipped a beat and she became a puddle of tears on the floor when she saw that her application status was incomplete. Her file indicated that her SAT scores and high school transcripts had not been received even though we had a confirmation the day before that both had been sent. Victoria was so upset she could not even think, so I tried to help her problem solve. We immediately sent an email to her college advisor in the hope she would respond quickly. Additionally, we contacted the SAT office and tried to get a verbal confirmation. Her advisor did email us back within a couple of hours confirming that her records had been sent, but we could not get a verbal commitment from the SAT office until the next business day. In the end, all of her application components had been submitted on time, but living through those few hours, fearing the unknown, was hell for both of us.

Receiving Notification

Whether a student applies RD, ED, EDI, EDII, EA, EA single choice, EA restrictive, priority, rolling admissions or VIP, each university notifies students a little differently. Most colleges inform the student directly via email and then follow up with a letter in the mail. Check each university for timing and method of contact.

Decision time is, without a doubt, very difficult for the college-bound senior (and for their parents), but it can be excruciating when it is unclear how and when your student will receive an answer from a university. The real stress factor that comes into play is when a student does not pay attention to the difference between those two-letter words, **"on"** and **"by."** Just identifying whether decisions will be delivered **"on"** or **"by"** a particular date can help ease the apprehension that comes with the waiting.

Those applications that inform students they will receive a decision **on** a particular day, typically mean all decisions, acceptances, deferrals or denials, will be sent out to all students on that one day. Colleges that send out decisions **by** a particular day often send decisions, acceptances, deferrals or denials out to various groups of students in waves throughout the application process. Each college may have a system in place that determines who hears when, but to the jittery 17-year-old, it is a source of angst.

REALITY CHECK

The days of receiving an acceptance letter in the mail on the same day as everyone else are long gone. The vast majority of schools notify students through email and usually only admitted or wait-listed students receive a formal letter. When Patrick applied EA to a few colleges. He interpreted one university's decision deadline of "by December 15" to mean "on December 15." When friends and acquaintances from different circles began receiving their decisions from the same university and he had not, his anxiety went into overdrive. He checked his email constantly and went on numerous websites to try to interpret the silence. He tried to figure out whether there was any pattern to the institution's notifications. Did they send out only acceptance letters? Did they review applications by geography, school or date of receipt? I think he would agree that it did, for a short time, drive him mad. (Although social media may have had some positive effects on the college process, from my perspective it has elevated the anxiety levels of seniors in high school by making all positive and negative information available instantaneously.) If he had had the forethought to question what the "by December 15" meant in terms of how applications are reviewed, it would have alleviated so much distress. Unfortunately, we went through much of the same ordeal in the spring. Initially, Patrick looked ahead knowing that by April 1 the waiting game would be over. By the second week of March, classmates started to receive RD responses from different universities. It seemed that Patrick would come home every day with news that another school had released its decisions. Some colleges send their decisions sooner than expected while others wait until the April 1 deadline. Looking back, I don't think he could have escaped the pressure he felt because all of his classmates were so consumed by the finality of the process. It might have helped, though, if we better understood the nuances of the college notification process.

Notification

The majority of university decisions are emailed to students on the date the school has designated. Not all decisions are followed up with a letter. Notifications are based upon when the application was submitted. Responses include the following: Admitted, Deferred, Denied, Wait-listed.

A. Admitted

1) An offer of admission will be electronically posted and/or mailed to a student on or by the date specified according to the individual university's website. Most often, email notifications are followed up with a letter via the U.S. Postal Service.

2) An offer of admission may come with a contingency. This relatively new phenomenon offers students admission to the university at a later date. This may include second semester enrollment or a semester/year abroad before attending a university. This unique approach not only benefits the students who want to commit to a particular university but also enables colleges to minimize the impact of students leaving while maintaining a steady enrollment of qualified candidates.

REALITY CHECK

For you and your student, there is nothing like opening an email or letter and reading the words, "Admitted to the Class of 20XX"! There is joy, just sheer joy! When it happens, celebrate. Go ahead, scream and jump up and down! You both deserve it! Even if the school is not a top choice, recognize the relief and confidence it brings your child. College is now a reality.

One situation we did not anticipate occurred when a notification came for Patrick from a distinguished university that was a part of the New England Small College Athletic Conference (NESCAC). The envelope was addressed to Patrick Clark, but when he opened it up, it read, "Congratulations John Smith! You have been accepted to XYZ University!" Confused and concerned, Patrick called the college immediately. A message was taken and relayed to the dean of admissions. Within five minutes, the dean called Patrick back, apologized, confirmed his acceptance and suggested that he and John Smith be roommates!

I feel that it is important to say that if students are accepted to a college that they know they will definitely not attend, it is best for them to notify the university as soon as possible. This shows consideration for the school as well as for the deferred and wait-listed students who are anxiously awaiting feedback.

B. Deferred

1) A student's application is usually only deferred during the early decision (ED) or early action (EA) process.

2) A student is usually informed electronically on or by the date specified for the individual university's ED or EA program. Most often, deferred applicant notification emails are not followed up with a letter.

3) A deferred response means that students have not been accepted in the first round of the review, but their applications will be looked at again during the regular decision (RD) process.

4) Deferred applicants will be notified about the status of their applications according to the regular decision (RD) parameters. They will be informed electronically and/or traditionally through the mail on or by the date specified by the individual university's RD guidelines.

5) Remember, a deferred application can provide students an opportunity to voice their interest and enthusiasm for an institution by following up with the Regional Coordinator and asking their high school college counselors to advocate for them.

C. Denied

1) A denied application at any stage in the admissions process means that a student will not be admitted to that particular university for the following fall semester.

2) A denied application during the early decision (ED) or early action (EA) stage does not allow the student to reapply for admission under regular decision (RD) for that year.

3) If a student is denied during regular decision there is typically no recourse for that particular year.

4) Any student denied acceptance to any university may reapply the following year.

REALITY CHECK

Denials come in many forms. The easy ones are those that come from a college students knew was a reach but thought it was worth a shot. The difficult ones are those that come from schools students feel strongly connected to and where they believe they had met the criteria for admission. Even if tears do not flow, recognize that this is a blow to your student's confidence and self-worth. Even though there is very little comfort a parent can offer, remember your child will be fine. By the time most students make their final college choices, they have often forgotten about that rejection and may even joke about it. Denial hurts but the wound heals and our teens move on.

D. Wait-Listed

1) Students are normally wait-listed during regular decision (RD).

2) Wait-listed students often have met the academic criteria for a given university but the college may not have enough space or believe they have other candidates that may be better suited to the university.

3) Students will be asked whether or not they would like to stay on the wait list. A response is required.

4) Wait-listed students can be offered admission up until the start of classes in the fall but the majority of offers come during May and early June.

5) Wait-listed candidates are usually admitted when the yield of accepted students does not fill the available class space. When there are more students who do not accept an offer of admission from a particular institution, there will be more opportunity for students to be moved off the wait list.

6) A student who is wait-listed and is highly interested in attending that university should immediately contact the college's Regional Coordinator to express this and write an email or letter reiterating the sentiment.

7) Students should contact their high school college counselors to discuss the likelihood of any movement off the wait list in order to get a true sense of their prospects. A high school counselor often has a very good idea of what to expect given past experiences with these universities. From the time an application is wait-listed, there is much jockeying for position among those candidates waiting for a response. Since movement is based upon whether or not other students send back their acceptances, it can be very unpredictable.

8) Students should ask their college counselors to advocate on their behalf if they are truly interested in attending the college that placed them on the waiting list. Many college counselors have relationships with university representatives, and verbal commitments from students could push those applications off the wait list. Remember, universities do want to accept good students who want to attend.

9) The vast number of wait-listed candidates is notified of acceptance by the first few days of May. If a student has already committed to one institution and subsequently is moved off the wait list of another more desirable university in May or June, the former university will usually release him or her from the contract but the student may forfeit the initial deposit. In order to resolve this dilemma in an honorable and legal way, seek the advice of your student's college counselor and research the protocol and policy of the individual university.

10) If students know for sure they won't be attending the university that wait-listed them, they should inform that college as soon as possible in order for the university to reevaluate their class and give other eager applicants the opportunity to attend.

REALITY CHECK

A quite impressive young man I have known since he was in first grade worked tirelessly throughout high school in order to secure a coveted admissions spot at a prestigious university. He applied to a number of schools ED, EA and RD. He was offered admission to many of his choices with scholarships but was wait-listed at his dream university. He spoke to his guidance counselor as soon as he heard and she followed up with the university on his behalf. As the decision date approached, he waited patiently to see if there was any movement from his number one choice and he made a contingency plan just in case. On April 29, the day he was going to commit to another university, his phone rang in the middle of his Chinese class. It was Duke calling. He was taken off the wait list and was admitted! He is still a proud Blue Devil but now a graduate.

Commitment

Commitment to a university by a student typically includes a written document or contract that requires the signature of the student as well the parents accompanied by an enrollment fee. The following are guidelines that pertain to a commitment:

1) The universal deadline for the admitted student to inform a university of a decision when filing under early action (EA) and regular decision (RD) is typically May 1. For the most part, an enrollment form and a confirmation fee are due. Since there are always exceptions, please refer to the university's website to confirm each deadline.

2) Early decision applications are binding agreements once submitted, so a student is already committed to that institution upon receipt of an offer of admission. The official commitment typically occurs from mid-December through mid-January.

3) The vast majority of universities send their financial aid packages with a letter of acceptance in order for students and their families to fully evaluate the merits of the offer. If one is not included when an offer of admission is given, it will most often be made available prior to the commitment date.

4) Students who have committed to schools regular decision and then change their minds about attending will most likely be released from the admissions contract but deposits may not be reimbursed. It is important to recognize that this may impact a students' future desire to attend that university if circumstances change. Again, in order to handle this dilemma in an honorable manner, seek the advice of the college guidance counselor and research the protocol and policy of the individual university.

CHAPTER 6

REALITY CHECK

All universities require commitments by May 1. This means that students secure their spots in the freshman class by submitting an agreement and a deposit of approximately $500–$1,000. Tuition payments are typically not required in full until sometime in August or the first day of classes. Between May 1 and August 1, students can nullify their college commitments. (That is how students are moved off a wait list.) If students revoke a commitment before tuition is due or classes begin, they may lose initial deposits. If they rescind the commitment once classes have begun, they will minimally be liable for the costs associated with that semester.

Deferring Admission

The process of deferring admission arises when students have gone through the college application process, have been accepted to a university but have for various reasons decided to wait another year or so before joining the student body. The following provides details associated with this option:

1) Most often, freshman, transfer students and re-admitted applicants are eligible to apply for deferment. All requests are reviewed on an individual basis.

2) Students may apply for deferred admission once they have been accepted and their deposits have been received.

3) All deferral forms must be completed by the date published by the university in order to be considered for placement in the following year's class. A university may allow a student to apply for deferment until the first day of school.

4) The length of time a student may be allowed to defer enrollment depends upon the university. Since it can range from a single to multiple semesters, the student should check the university's policy.

5) Accepted students who decide to defer admission should formally submit a letter in writing to the dean of admissions stating the rationale for the delay. Requests are often made due to illness or military, religious and humanitarian service, or to experience a GAP Year. (See Chapter 11 for more on a GAP Year.) Supporting documentation may be required with an application for deferment.

6) A deferred admission request may not always be approved. Individual colleges vary in their policies and procedures as to what is considered an appropriate reason to grant a request but as GAP years become more common, universities seem more open and flexible.

7) Any deferred admission request can have financial consequences so students should explore the monetary implications of the petition.

8) Students should seek the advice and guidance of their high school college counselors when exploring or initiating deferment.

athletics

STEP #1

Accept that college sports are a business.

STEP #2

Expect varying degrees of sports competition in college.

STEP #3

Recognize that level I sports programs are selective and are subject to the rules and regulations of a collegiate governing body including the National Collegiate Athletic Association (NCAA), the Association of Intercollegiate Athletics (NAIA) and the National Junior College Athletic Association (NJCAA).

STEP #4

Know level II programs include intramurals sports, which are open to all students, and club sports, which can be very selective, competitive and require travel.

STEP #5

Understand that in the NCAA only Division I and Division II colleges offer athletic scholarships while Division III colleges do not.

STEP #6

Recognize the NAIA does offer athletic scholarships.

STEP #7

Know the NJCAA may offer grant-in-aid to athletes as long as the student has been admitted to the institution.

STEP #8

Accept that it is unlikely most high school athletes will play a college sport; only 3.4% of all male high school basketball athletes play in the NCAA.

STEP #9

Remember that less than two percent of high school athletes win sports scholarships every year at NCAA colleges and universities. The average scholarship during 2017 for men is $6,283 and for women is $7,541.[1]

STEP #10

Know that Ivy League schools do not offer athletic scholarships. All aid is based upon need.

STEP #11

Understand that universities that do not offer sports scholarships are able to give grants to a student or athlete they are pursuing, but that aid is not guaranteed for four years.

STEP #12

Know that universities that only provide need-based financial aid may choose to offer grants to a student or athlete they are pursuing, but that aid is also not guaranteed for all four years.

STEP #13

Acknowledge that Division I coaches seek to recruit only elite athletes.

STEP #14

Remember that many prestigious schools have a formula called the academic index which they use to help determine if a student-athlete is a good candidate.

STEP #15

Assume that athletics may help students gain admission into more prestigious institutions, but that does not necessarily mean they will receive financial aid or scholarships.

STEP #16

Realize it is not uncommon for athletes to take a post graduate (PG) year after high school to further their skills or play at a junior college to earn a spot on a DI team later on.

Sports in College

Sports in college can include a variety of options for the high school athlete. The opportunities to participate can be broken down into two levels. **Level I** includes sports that are subject to the rules and regulations of a collegiate governing body including the National Collegiate Athletic Association (NCAA), the Association of Intercollegiate Athletics (NAIA) and the National Junior College Athletic Association (NJCAA). This first level is often differentiated by selective participation since only the best athletes are chosen to compete. It is estimated that, nationally, 615,000 athletes are currently playing under these sanctioned team umbrellas. **Level II** includes club and intramural sports. Individual sports at this level may have an administration overseeing them, such as the National Club Baseball Association, LLC (NCBA). As a rule, club teams are pretty structured, requiring students to dedicate significant time, while intramurals tend to be more relaxed and more about recreation.

Level I

Amateur, competitive athletes in the U.S. may well find themselves playing college sports. If so, the universities offering an undergraduate education offer sports programs that fall into five different categories for more than 30 sports. Three of these divisions are housed under the NCAA, while the NAIA and the NJCAA manage the others. The following is a brief synopsis of the principles of each organization:

I. NATIONAL COLLEGIATE ATHLETIC ASSOCIATION (NCAA)

The mission of the NCAA "is to be an integral part of higher education and to focus on the development of our student-athletes."[2]

Participation levels at NCAA championship sports are rising, but "of the 8 million students currently participating in high school athletics in the United States, only 480, 000 of them will compete at NCAA schools."[3]

According to the NCAA website as recently as December 2018, "The likelihood of an NCAA athlete earning a college degree is significantly greater; graduation success rates for 86% in Division I, 71% in Division II and 87% in Division III."[4]

Although these trends are positive, the reality is that a small percentage of high school athletes will play sports in college. For probability estimates by sport for high school athletes in the NCAA, go to www.ncaa.org/about/resources/research/estimated-probability-competing-college-athletics.

A. NCAA DIVISION I *(DI)*

NCAA Division I colleges are considered the most competitive institutions among the three divisions. They are typically larger institutions with generous student populations that choose to dedicate more financial resources to support athletics. They are often able to accomplish this due to the extensive media contracts that Division I conferences attract. (Especially football and basketball) The exception to this may be the

Ivy League Division I schools which do not utilize media contracts and endowments to give athletic scholarships but admit student-athletes on a need-blind basis. This means if student-athletes are accepted, they will receive financial assistance based upon what they can afford to contribute. The following is a summary of the attributes specific to DI sports:

1) Division I has approximately **350 colleges** and universities in its membership.

2) Division I includes over **6,000 athletic teams**.

3) Division I has approximately **179,000 student-athletes**.

4) Division I **offers scholarships** to athletes but they may not be guaranteed for all four years.

5) Division I **offers financial aid** to athletes but it also may not be guaranteed for all four years.

6) Division I schools typically have the highest **athletic budgets**, but only 59% of all student-athletes receive some level of athletic aid versus 62% at Division II and 80% at Division III.

7) Division I incoming student-athletes must be **certified as amateurs**.

8) Division I first year student-athletes have taken **core course requirements** and maintained a minimum GPA in order to be eligible to play and receive scholarships.

9) Division I athletes are usually **recruited under NCAA policies**. Rules governing how and when a prospect can be contacted differ from sport to sport. This includes time frames that are identified as contact period, dead period, evaluation period and quiet period. For more information, go to www.ncaa.org/student-athletes/resources/recruiting-calendars?division=d1.

10) A student-athlete may **visit a college** in an official or unofficial capacity. Rules governing how often and for how long a prospect can visit a college differ from sport to sport. See the NCAA website at www.ncaa.org.

11) An **Official Student Athletic Visit** to a Division I college also requires students and their high schools to file forms with the NCAA Eligibility Center. These forms are used to confirm students' academic eligibility for college based upon the core courses required and the standards set by the NCAA. To register, visit web3.ncaa.org/ecwr3/.

12) Division I student-athletes must **sign a letter of intent** with an individual university when they agree to attend. This contract will detail the terms of their agreement. For more information, go to www.nationalletter.org.

13) **Division I football is the only sport that is subdivided** based upon sponsorship. The three divisions are the Football Bowl Subdivision, the Football Championship Subdivision and the All Other DI Subdivision.

14) For a list of **NCAA Division I** sports, go to www.ncaa.org/championships?division=d1.

15) For a list of NCAA Division I members, go to web3.ncaa.org/directory/.

REALITY CHECK

If your son or daughter is a high level athlete, you may have already been contacted by some college coaches. In the NCAA Division I, this is typically done through the club team circuit or a high school coach. There are many rules and regulations regarding recruiting, but a good rule of thumb to go by is, prior to their junior year, a college cannot approach athletes through their high school coaches but can unofficially approach them if the connection has been made through a club team. NCAA Division I schools may start to commit top athletes when they are rising juniors. This means that during the summer between sophomore and junior years, NCAA Division I coaches may look to recruit the vast majority of athletes. These coaches are actively searching to fill their rosters two years down the road and will continue to monitor the progress of their potential recruits as well as explore new talent. When there is mutual interest between an athlete and a university, there is typically a verbal commitment with the caveat that the athlete stays healthy and maintains a certain grade level. Even though NCAA Division I athletes are required to sign a letter of intent, the actual signing of an athlete for most Division I universities typically does not take place any sooner than the fall of senior year. My tenacious, astute niece was only a junior in high school that December when she verbally committed to play soccer at a DI college. She had attended soccer showcases since sophomore year in high school and began fielding offers from DI schools in the fall of junior year. Her verbal commitment was made in concert with her parents and the college coach but did not include any written communication. She did not sign her Letter of Intent with that university until February of senior year. Her diligence and hard work at academics and sports have paid off since she is a freshman student-athlete at her dream Division I university.

My first voyage into DI college sports came when my son Patrick toyed with the idea of rowing in college. He started rowing as a sophomore in high school because his older sister influenced him, he was bored with more traditional sports and he wanted to broaden his social network outside of his small high school. To his surprise, he loved the physical challenges and comradery of the sport. As he progressed, his interest grew and he became very competitive. When it came time to decide whether he would pursue this interest in college, he was initially ambivalent due to the time commitment. As he progressed through junior year of high school, his opinion waffled on whether or not he should pursue rowing, but as a rising senior, Patrick caught crew fever and furiously attacked this sport. In mid-October, he managed to earn a coveted seat in a four-man boat for the prestigious Head of the Charles Regatta in Boston. To the surprise of his coaches, his boat placed 11th out of 86 world-wide entrants after only three days of practice. This placement actually elevated him to a high-level status as a rower, but, as we discovered, it was too late for him to talk to any of the DI schools he was interested in about rowing for them. He was able to continue dialog with some Division III schools and ultimately gained acceptance at some of them, but his hope to compete at some of the more celebrated Division I schools never materialized. By mid- to late October, these Division I schools had already firmed up their recruits for the next fall's admission and were looking two years out. Patrick did continue to row throughout his senior year in high school but ultimately chose not to row in college. He is still happily pursuing his true passion, music, at NYU Steinhardt Graduate School after earning bachelor's degrees in Music and Business at Tulane University.

B. NCAA DIVISION II *(DII)*

NCAA Division II colleges can be just as competitive and the athletes just as proficient as at Division I schools, but Division II institutions may not have the revenue to support, or choose not to place, such a large financial commitment on sports. Athough smaller colleges compete at Division II level, the real focus of Division II sports is to fully engage the student-athlete in the real campus experience. "Student-athletes are recognized for their academic success, athletics contributions and campus/community involvement."[5] Following are some defining factors about DII sports:

1) Division II includes **300 colleges** in its membership.

2) Division II has **25 active conferences in 45 states**.

3) Division II engages approximately **121,000 student-athletes**; 58% male, 42% female.

4) Division II **does offer partial scholarships and financial aid** to student-athletes.

5) Division II incoming student-athletes must be **certified as amateurs**.

6) A Division II student-athlete may **visit a college** in an official or unofficial capacity.

7) An **Official Student Athletic Visit** to a Division II college also requires students and their high schools to file forms with the NCAA Eligibility Center. These forms are used to confirm the students' academic eligibility for college based upon the core courses required and the standards set by the NCAA. To register, visit web3.ncaa.org/ecwr3/.

8) Division II **athletes are often recruited** under NCAA policies. Rules governing how and when a prospect can be contacted differ from sport to sport. For details, go to www.ncaa.org/student-athletes/resources/recruiting-calendars?division=d2.

9) Division II student-athletes may **sign a letter of intent** with an individual university when they agree to attend a Division II college. This contract will detail the terms of their agreement. For more information, go to www.nationalletter.org

10) For a list of **NCAA Division II sports**, go to web3.nccaa.org/directory/.

11) For more information regarding the **NCAA Division II**, go to www.ncaa.org/about?division=d2.

REALITY CHECK

NCAA Division II sports are found across the country but tend to be less visible than the many NCAA DI or even some DIII schools. DII schools promote the fact that they offer a better balance between academics, sports and campus life than Division I universities. DII schools do offer another choice for those high school athletes who wish to continue to play a sport they enjoy in a well-rounded, though still highly competitive environment.

C. DIVISION III *(DIII)*

The philosophy of the "Colleges and universities in Division III place the highest priority on the overall quality of the educational experience and on the successful completion of all students' academic programs. They seek to establish and maintain an environment in which a student-athlete's athletics activities are conducted as an integral part of the student-athlete's educational experience, and an environment that values cultural diversity and gender equity among their student-athletes and athletics staff."[6] Limited coaching time, shorter practices, a condensed playing season and regional competition that reduces time away from campus keep these student-athletes focused on their studies. A Division III athlete will experience a competitive playing field and should look to become integrated into the college campus, community and life. Here are the facts:

1) Division III has **450 colleges** and universities in its membership.

2) Division III fields over **190,000 student-athletes**, while offering 28 national championships.

3) Division III **does not offer athletic scholarships**.

4) Division III institutions **may offer grants** for academic aptitude or accomplishments to athletes but they are not necessarily extended for all four years of college.

5) Division III **does offer financial aid** to all eligible students. According to the NCAA website, 80% of all DIII student-athletes receive some form of academic grant or need-based scholarships.

6) Division III incoming student-athletes **do not need to be certified as amateurs** and **do not need to register with the NCAA Eligibility Center.**

7) Division III athletes **can be recruited** by coaches but there are no formal agreements or contracts; the athletes must still submit their college applications to the institution and are subject to the same admission standards as all candidates.

8) Division III athletes **may get verbal commitments from a college coach before their applications have been processed**, but be aware that a definitive acceptance is not valid until it is received in writing.

9) Athletes may **visit** a Division III college but must do so in an unofficial manner, providing their own transportation and staying with current athletes.

10) Division III **coaches have limited contact** with student-athletes in and out of season. How much time a coach can spend with a team differs from sport to sport. These parameters are set and governed by the NCAA.

11) Division III sports often have **captains' practices** in or out of season. These practices are run by team captains, are designed to keep the team on track and often bridge the training gap between seasons or provide a needed, extra session.

12) For a list of **NCAA Division III sports**, go to http://www.ncaa.org/championships?division=d3.

13) For more information about the **NCAA Division III sports**, go to www.ncaa.org/about?division=d3.

REALITY CHECK

Division III college coaches do evaluate rising juniors and dub some as athletes to watch, but most do not approach students or firm up any commitments until they are rising seniors. This means that the summer between junior and senior years is when the vast majority of Division III colleges begin to verbally commit athletes. (Many coaches ask students for SAT/ACT test scores and transcripts before making verbal commitments.) Since Division III athletes do not sign a contract with a university to play a sport, they must rely on a coach's word. They must go about the business of filing applications and maintaining grades and fitness before they can be accepted to that university. (Most Division III athletes apply early decision to the college they have verbally committed to.) A recruited athlete may receive a letter of acceptance a week or two in advance of the early decision candidates, but this is not always the case. It is extremely important to note that acceptance to a university is never official until a student receives a letter of acceptance. In some instances, verbal commitments with a coach are not always honored. For various reasons, some athletes who thought they had secured placement in a particular college because of a coach's feedback were surprised to discover they had been deferred or denied admission.

Athletics can be the key to admission and even to receiving grants at some highly selective, DIII schools. A competitive DIII school may use a formula called the academic index which helps them determine if a student-athlete is a good candidate. The academic index considers students' standardized test scores (SAT or ACT and Subject Tests) and their GPAs. If students do not meet the index requirements, they will probably not be admitted to the university regardless of athletic ability. A very bright, athletic family friend was admitted to one of the top liberal arts colleges in the country where she played soccer for four years. For her hard work on and off the field, she was awarded a grant her freshman and sophomore years. This was a welcome surprise for her hard-working parents.

My first experience with DIII college sports came from crew with Aly. As I previously mentioned, my older daughter wanted to row in college. Since this criterion was not negotiable in our college search, we worked our way through the mine field of DI, DII and DIII programs, ultimately concentrating our focus on DIII schools. Eventually, Aly narrowed her choices to just two colleges that she was considering applying to early decision. On Sunday, November 15, which was ED due day, Aly sat in the family room making a list of the pros and cons of each school. I clearly had an opinion as to which school I thought would be the better fit for her, but I was adamant about not influencing her decision. (Fortunately, I did believe that both options could work for her but felt more strongly about one.) We talked that afternoon, but mostly I tried to listen. Throughout the day, I asked questions to help her determine if she could see which way she should go. It was a difficult choice because one school was lobbying heavily for her to apply, but it seemed to me something was holding her back. It did surprise me that a question I posed about the coaches was the one that sealed the deal for her. Since crew was going to be a big part of the college experience for Aly, it was important to her that there was chemistry between the coach and her. Aly remembered that the crew coach at one of the colleges had asked her a question that had taken her aback. She had asked, "Would this school still be the right place for you if crew did not work out?" This was the first and only coach who had actually shown an outward interest in Aly beyond what she could do for the team. She ended up choosing to apply ED to this school, and as it turns out, her instinct about the coach was right. Crew has been an extraordinarily demanding sport but her experience with the William Smith Crew Team has enabled

Aly to grow and mature. Even though it has been challenging, Aly and I agree that this college and crew team were the right choice and best fit for her.

II NATIONAL ASSOCIATION OF INTERCOLLEGIATE ATHLETICS (NAIA)

"The National Association of Intercollegiate Athletics (NAIA), headquartered in Kansas City, Mo., is a governing body of small athletics programs that are dedicated to character-driven intercollegiate athletics."[7] The focus of NAIA schools is on the student-athlete's success on and off the field. The NAIA member colleges, primarily located in the Midwest, tend to be smaller and offer fewer sports than the school members of the NCAA. Since the NAIA is grouped into conferences organized by several factors besides performance, skill level and competition can vary significantly. The following facts are indicative of NAIA sports:

1) NAIA fields **65,000 student-athletes**.

2) NAIA participates in **17 sports and 25 national championships**.

3) NAIA membership includes more than **250 colleges** and universities in the U.S. and Canada.

4) NAIA governs **21 conferences**.

5) NAIA offers $600 million in **athletic scholarships.**

6) Individual NAIA schools **offer financial aid**, scholarships, grant-in-aid and loans.

7) All NAIA prospective student-athletes must be deemed **eligible** to play a sport. Go to www.playnaia.org.

8) **NAIA athletes are often recruited.** NAIA rules governing contact between an athlete and a coach tend to be less restrictive.

9) **NAIA prospects may visit** a college. Any tryout must occur on campus for a maximum of two days. Policies for reimbursement of a visit vary by institution.

10) The NAIA **doescs not have a letter of intent program.** Individual NAIA schools may offer athletes letters of intent, which are not binding, but are recognized by other institutions within a conference.

11) For more information and a **list of NAIA sports**, go to www.naia.org.

III NATIONAL JUNIOR COLLEGE ATHLETIC ASSOCIATION (NJCAA)

The NJCAA serves as the national governing body for two-year College athletics in the United States. Founded in 1937 at Fresno, California, its purpose is to foster a national program of athletic participation in an environment that supports equitable opportunities consistent with the educational objectives of member colleges. "In April of 2016, the NJCAA Board of Directors approved a new strategic plan for the association titled UNIFIED IN THE PURSUIT OF EXCELLENCE. The new strategic plan centers on five goals: Educational Opportunities, Data Research, National Standards

& Accountability, Competition Structure, Marketing, Branding & Promotion of the NJCAA."[8] The following highlights the major aspects of the NJCAA:

1) The NJCAA has **300 two-year colleges** in its membership.

2) The NJCAA fields approximately **60,000 student-athletes** each year.

3) The NJCAA competes in **25 different sports while offering some Division I, II and III competition**.

4) The NJCAA organization is broken down geographically into **24 regions across the country** and does offer the opportunity for national championship play.

5) The NJCAA is affiliated with **22 sports organizations** such as the U.S.A. Basketball and the U.S. Olympic Committee, providing nationwide exposure.

6) The NJAA **may offer grant-in-aid to athletes** as long as they have been admitted to the institution. These offers may not be available for both years of study.

7) NJCAA incoming student-athletes **must be certified as amateurs** in order to be considered eligible to play. For more information on eligibility, go to www.njcaa.org/eligibility/index.

8) NJCAA **student-athletes may visit a junior college**. A paid visit requires the stay to be a maximum of two days and two nights, limiting access to the college campus and local community.

9) NJCAA **student-athletes can be recruited** under the policies and procedures of the organization.

10) NJCAA student-athletes may **sign a letter of intent** with an individual school when they agree to attend. It is awarded for a maximum of one year and must be signed during the time frame allowed.

11) For more information and a **list of NJCAA sports**, go to www.njcaa.org.

REALITY CHECK

Junior colleges are also used as a tool by many athletes to move into a more competitive college and professional environment. Athletes who want to play competitive sports in college may attend a junior college in the hopes of being noticed by an NCAA or NAIA college coach. This strategy has worked well for many including football cornerback, Malcolm Butler. I hadn't heard of this mysterious rookie until the last few seconds of Super Bowl XLIX when he intercepted a pass to win the game for the New England Patriots. Did you know that Malcolm started his career at Hines Community College in Raymond, Mississippi? Who knew that you could start a college football career at a community college and end up making the clutch play to win the 2015 Super Bowl?

Level II

I. CLUB SPORTS

Collegiate club sports offer an opportunity for students to continue to play and compete in a sport that they are passionate. It can also provide an opportunity for students to try out for a sport they have wanted to experience. Club sports allow students to develop leadership, organizational and decision-making skills while meeting the challenges associated with competition and performance. Here are some facts:

1) Club Sports typically **do not meet as frequently** or for as long as varsity sports.

2) Club Sports **can be very demanding and highly competitive** depending upon the sport and the university.

3) Club Sports usually **have tryouts and cuts.**

4) Club Sports are, most often, run by **students.**

5) Club Sports have **scheduled practices and games.**

6) Members are **often required to fundraise.**

7) Club Sports provide instruction for **player development.**

8) Club Sports may **charge dues of a nominal amount** for participation.

9) Club Sports typically have a **coach.**

10) Club Sports are usually **supported by the university**, which provides office support as well as access to facilities and equipment.

11) Club Sport **funding** for travel, competition, equipment and participation fees are often supplemented by the university.

12) Club sports are often a **part of a league** which may offer the opportunity for a championship.

13) Club sport **leagues may be regional or national**, depending upon the sport and the institution.

14) In 2009, **The National Federation of Collegiate Club Sports Leagues, LLC,** or CollClubSports, was formed in order to provide services and an infrastructure to a broad array of collegiate sports clubs. In 2018, CollClubSports includes baseball, softball, football and basketball.

15) For **more information** on the National Federation of Collegiate Club Sports Leagues, LLC, go to www.collclubsports.com.

REALITY CHECK

My good natured, spirited niece played competitive soccer throughout middle school and high school. She knew she did not want to make soccer a significant part of her college experience so she chose not to pursue it. But once she was on campus as a freshman, she decided to look into club soccer. She tried out and made the team which competes in the Southeast

Collegiate Soccer Alliance-North Division. There is a coach, the dues are $50 for the year, practice is twice a week, there are one or two games a week, and overnight travel is not typical. Overall, she is very happy with her decision to play club soccer. Some of her closest friends are teammates, and she has been able to meet and become friends with some upperclassmen which really helped when she rushed for a sorority.

II. INTRAMURAL SPORTS

Intramural sports programs offer students the opportunity to participate in a variety of sports in a friendly, flexible environment. The goal of intramural sports is to promote a healthy lifestyle by encouraging social interaction and skill development in a somewhat competitive environment. Intramural sports can add so much to a college experience by offering comradery, structure and fitness in a non-threatening manner. The facts about collegiate intramural sports:

1) Intramural sports are typically **open to the students, faculty and employees** of a university.
2) Intramural sports are **played on campus**.
3) Intramural sports usually **do not require tryouts or have cuts**.
4) Intramural teams **may be divided by skill** level if there are enough players to do so.
5) Intramural sports **meet one to two times a week** for practices and games.
6) Intramural **games are usually just for fun**.
7) The **university provides the facilities and equipment** for intramural sports.
8) The infrastructure of intramural sports is most often **run by the recreation office of the university**.
9) **Team captains** typically run the practices.
10) A **nominal fee** is charged to join a team.
11) **Intramural sports vary by school** but often include the following: badminton, basketball, soccer, volleyball, dodge ball, flag football, ice hockey, floor hockey, kickball, ping pong, softball, squash, table tennis, tennis, ultimate Frisbee and Wiffle ball.

REALITY CHECK FOR ALL ATHLETICS

It is essential for you and your student to remember that sports in college is a business. Make sure your college-bound DI athlete understands this. The financial implications for a university, based upon whether a team is doing well, are tremendous. From alumni support to endowment to media contracts, the pendulum can swing ether way depending upon wins and losses.

In a 60 Minutes story about Nick Saban, head football coach for the University of Alabama, Chancellor Robert Witt said that Saban was "the best financial investment the University has ever made." At that time, Saban's record of 72 wins and only nine losses over six seasons at University of Alabama had financially impacted the university in such a positive way that nothing else could meet or surpass it. Can you imagine the excitement of the new Chancellor at University of Alabama, Ray Hayes, over Saban's continuing winning record of 145 wins and only 20 losses since 2007!

FOOTNOTE: POST GRADUATE (PG) YEAR OR GAP YEAR

A post graduate (PG) and a gap year are often used interchangeably to reference the year or two after high school when a student takes some time off before attending college. Although a student may choose to take a PG or a gap year after high school for several reasons, a PG year for sports has its own implications. Many high school student-athletes take a PG year to position themselves as better candidates for athletics in college. (Many athletes also choose to attend a junior college aspiring to be recruited by an NCAA or NAIA coach.) Athletes may choose to attend a preparatory school continuing to play their sport in the hopes of catching the eye of a coach at a coveted university. These students may also be trying to improve their grades and academic standings to get into a selective college. (A college coach may even advise a student to do so in order to gain admission to their university.)

REALITY CHECK

Playing in a junior league after high school is very common for hockey players, but it is a risky proposition because there are no guarantees that the student will be picked up by a college. In my large extended family, two hockey-playing students have explored the junior league route. In both cases, it was difficult to earn a spot on the team and expensive to remain there. One of them, a fine, soft-spoken young man, worked tirelessly for three years before he was recruited by a DIII college. The other, a quick-witted, easy-going guy, played two years on a junior league team before he committed to a DIII college. It is not uncommon for hockey players to find themselves playing in a junior league for one, two or even three years. (Hockey may be more challenging than other sports since many colleges only select players who are at least 19-years-old. My family members were both just 17 when they graduated from high school.) Fortunately, these young men are determined to pursue college degrees, but the reality is that many of these athletes lose interest in the academic side of the game if they are not selected or stay away from academia long enough. When I asked the first of these young men, a 21-year-old rising sophomore, if there was anything he would have done differently over the past four years, he said he would have maintained his honors GPA throughout senior year of high school and would have taken college classes while he was playing in the junior league so he could be further along in getting his degree. As you can see, there can be both positive and negative side effects for the student-athlete who starts college as a 20- or 21-year-old freshman.

Some athletes avoid a PG or gap year by transferring to a different high school during sophomore or junior year and repeating the grade they just completed. This is called "reclassing" and is very common because it gives student-athletes the chance to improve their play and their academics while maturing mentally and physically before any official high school graduation. Transferring is often used as a maneuver for a student-athlete to gain admittance to a prestigious college or to position an athlete for play in a higher division. There are even some high school/preparatory schools that specialize in a particular sport. In New Hampshire, there is a group of high/prep schools that focus on basketball. They are part of what is called the New England Preparatory School Athletic Council, Class AAA. On a quiet Friday night in an athletic facility nestled in the mountains on the campus of one of those schools, you are likely to find a college basketball coach sitting unnoticed in the stands because of the superb talent on the court. Relocating from one school to another has become even more popular in the past several years. I have personally witnessed this tactic employed many times and seen its effectiveness.

CHAPTER 8

overview of the financial aid process

STEP #1

Understand the cost and possible debt associated with financing a college education.

STEP #2

Identify the sources of financial aid including the federal government, the state government, individual colleges and nonprofit/private entities.

STEP #3

Determine eligibility for financial aid, including citizenship status, at the state and federal levels.

STEP #4

Determine your financial aid need by identifying your Expected Family Contribution (EFG):

$$Financial\ Aid\ Need =$$
$$Cost\ of\ Attendance\ (COA) - Expected\ Family\ Contribution\ (EFC)$$

Introduction

The college financial aid process can be complicated and confusing especially since it is constantly changing. I will be the first to admit that I am not an expert on the subject, but I have researched it and educated myself. What I hope to do in the following chapters is to simplify the process for you by providing pertinent information and some insight into the reality of financing a college education. Managing the financial side of a college education is stressful and challenging. I can still recall my own mother's dread and anxiety, 30 plus years ago, when she was attempting to fill out my college financial aid forms. I can easily visualize our kitchen table covered with reams of paper and boxes as my Mom, hunched over the forms, worked late into the night to complete them. At the time, it annoyed me that it always came down to the last possible minute before we submitted those forms, but now I can see that it was the bewildering aspects of the process that made her take so long. I hope the following facts will assist you in mastering the college financial aid process as it exits today but remember that various aspects of financial aid will change.

I. Cost and Possible Debt Associated with a College Education

"Student debt is still rising for bachelor's degree recipients. In 2016, seven in 10 graduating seniors at **public and private nonprofit colleges** had student loans. When they graduate, the average student loan borrower has $37,172 in student loans, a $20,000 increase from 13 years ago."[1] The national average student payment is $393 per month over the standard 10-year repayment plan. While interest rates on student loans, especially private ones, vary dramatically, federal and private college loans have risen to an all time high. According to the Federal Reserve, student debt now equates to $1.5 trillion, up more than 47 % over the past four years. "Over the last 20 years, inflation-adjusted published tuition and fees have more than doubled at four year public institutions and have increased by more than 50% at private four year and public two-year colleges."[2] As students take on more debt to attend public and private universities, they also take on more personal financial risk. One reason for the rising debt may be that it's fairly easy now to get federal college loans. The availability of federal funding may have also enabled universities to increase tuition and fees without impacting enrollment.

Depending on which side of the table you sit, there will always be debate over how much debt can and should be incurred by students and their families to pay for college. Recognize that even Federal Loan Servicers like Sallie Mae/Navient, Performant Financial, Expert Global Solutions, ECMC Group and Allied Interstate are running businesses; they exist to make money. The question you and your students should ask is, "How much debt is reasonable to incur throughout a college career?" (NOTE: Be aware that federal loan servers may also underwrite private student loans. Sallie Mae recently moved its federal loan services into a separate company called Navient while keeping the Sallie Mae entity for private loan services.)

REALITY CHECK

*Although the majority of Americans struggle to finance a college educa-
tion, the good news is that an undergraduate degree is still a good investment. According to the SCF (Survey of Consumer Finances), "data strongly
suggest that increases in the average lifetime incomes of college-educated
Americans have more than kept pace with increases in debt loads."[3] More
recently, opinion editorials and critics suggest that students from lower
income brackets may not fare as well ecomomically as middle class Americans due to access to higher paying jobs and student debt.*

*In order to help students understand the big financial picture of attend-
ing college, parents should initiate conversations with them about pro-
jected monthly payments and how much money they will need to earn in
order to live and repay these loans. These discussions are especially important if students are thinking of applying to private universities that usually
cost significantly more than public institutions. In my opinion, the amount
of debt a student can incur when attending a private university can far
exceed the average $37,172 in federal and private loans that was quoted
previously. The mere fact that a private college education can cost upwards
of $20,000–$30,000 more per year than a public one substantiates this
belief. Analyzing the financial implications of a college education with your
student will help them plan for a successful future before it even begins.*

II. Sources and Types of Financial Aid

Financial aid is money awarded to an individual to help pay for college or career
schools. Financial aid, which is used to cover tuition and living expenses, can be
sourced from the Federal Government, State Government, Individual Colleges or
Nonprofit/Private Entities. These organizations, which have their own terms and conditions, will be discussed in detail below.

There are several different types of financial aid one can receive from these institutions. The implications of these will also be addressed in detail later in this chapter.
The following summarizes the options:

- **Grants**—financial aid that does not typically have to be repaid.
- **Loans**—borrowed money for college costs that must be repaid with interest.
- **Work-study**—earned money from a work program that helps students pay for
  school.
- **Scholarships**—a financial award used to defray the costs of college; most often
  based on merit, need or an association with a particular group such as teachers or
  veterans; usually awarded for one year; typically does not have to be repaid.

III. Eligibility

Eligibility for any financial aid or scholarships depends on a set of parameters that must be met in order to receive an award. Here are the eligibility guidelines for each of the major entities providing funding for college.

A. Federal Financial Aid Eligibility

U.S. CITIZEN

The Federal conditions in order to receive financial aid are that you must:

a) Demonstrate **financial need** (for most programs);

b) Be a **U.S. citizen** or an eligible noncitizen (see below for noncitizen details);

c) Have a valid **Social Security number** (with the exception of students from the Republic of the Marshall Islands, Federated States of Micronesia or the Republic of Palau);

d) **Be registered** with Selective Service, if you're a male you must register between the ages of 18 and 25;

e) Have a **high school diploma**, General Education Development, GED, Certificate, or completed a homeschool approved education.

f) Be enrolled or accepted for enrollment as a **regular student** in an eligible degree or certificate program;

g) **Maintain satisfactory academic progress** in college or career school;

h) **Sign statements on the FAFSA** stating that you are not in default on a federal student loan and do not owe money on a federal student grant.[4]

NON U.S. CITIZEN

The Federal conditions for a non-citizen student must fall into one of the following categories:

a) U.S. National who was born in American Samoa or Swains Island,

b) "Have a GREEN CARD. You are eligible if you have a Form I-551, I-151, or I-551C, also known as a green card, showing you are a U.S. permanent resident

c) Have an ARRIVAL-DEPARTURE RECORD. Your Arrival-Departure Record (I-94) from U.S. Citizenship and Immigration Services must show one of the following:

   1) Refugee

   2) Asylum Granted

   3) Cuban-Haitian Entrant (Status Pending)

   4) Conditional Entrant (valid only if issued before April 1, 1980)

   5) Parolee

d) Have BATTERED IMMIGRANT STATUS. You are designated as a "battered immigrant-qualified alien" if you are a victim of abuse by your citizen or permanent resident spouse, or you are the child of a person designated as such under the Violence Against Women Act.

e) Have a T-VISA. You are eligible if you have a T-visa or a parent with a T-1 visa."[5]

B. State Financial Aid Eligibility

State financial aid programs are typically geared toward in-state students and often require a student to be a resident for a specific period of time, be enrolled as a student in an accredited career or degree program and plan to attend a state approved institution. Because eligibility requirements for scholarships, tuition waivers or loans vary within a given state, it is always best to check with the individual state university in order to insure you meet the requirements and deadlines. The U.S. Department of Education provides an Education Resource Organization Directory of the offices of Student Financial Assistance by state. The list provides the name, address, phone number and websites for each state's financial aid office. It can be found at www2.ed.gov/about/contacts/state/index.html.

REALITY CHECK

In order to receive any financial aid, including low interest or no interest loans, from the vast majority of states, you MUST submit a Free Application for Federal Student Aid (FAFSA). The following information details the requirements for a No Interest Loan (NIL) in the state of Massachusetts.

"To be eligible for a Massachusetts No Interest Loan, a student must:

1) *Be a permanent legal resident of Massachusetts for one year prior to the start of the academic year for which the loan is awarded.*

2) *Be a United States citizen or eligible non citizen under Title IV regulations.*

3) *Have applied for financial aid, using the standard Free Application for Federal Student Aid (FAFSA).*

4) *Be in compliance with Selective Service Registration Requirements.*

5) *Not be in default of any federal or state loans for attendance at any institution or owe a refund for any previous financial aid received.*

6) *Be enrolled full time (at least 12 credits or its equivalent) in a certificate, associate or bachelor's degree program at an eligible institution.*

7) *Not have received a prior bachelor's degree or its equivalent.*

8) *Be maintaining satisfactory academic progress in accordance with institutional and federal standards.*

9) *Demonstrate financial aid need as determined by the Federal Methodology need analysis criteria.*"[6]

C. Eligibility at Individual Colleges

Each individual college or university determines students' eligibility for financial aid. Most institutions base eligibility on financial need so it will use the information from a student's FAFSA to determine eligibility for federal or state programs. Since many schools also have their own financial aid programs that may be funded from other sources, such as endowments, a student should explore the university's website or contact the financial aid office independently to find out what type of aid is available. If eligible, a student not only needs to determine whether there are any additional forms required besides the FAFSA, but also needs to know the deadline for submission of these forms. **NOTE:** Some institutions may require the College Scholarship Service Financial Aid Profile (CSS/PROFILE) to assist them in determining financial aid. The CSS/PROFILE is an application distributed by the College Board that typically allows a student to apply for non-federal financial aid and scholarships. Financial aid packages vary by college based upon the cost of attending a university versus money available to distribute. For more information on the FAFSA, see Chapter #3. For more information on the CSS/PROFILE, see Chapter #10.

D. Eligibility for Nonprofit or Private Entities

Eligibility for any financial aid or scholarships coming from a source outside of the state or federal government often has very specific, individual requirements. Compliance may be related to a number of factors including financial need, academic achievement, military service, civic leadership, employment or community involvement. Since there are numerous options for students to pursue in the private sector, they should continue to research and discuss the opportunities and guidelines with a high school advisor, family members and community leaders. For more information on nonprofit and private entities, see Chapter #10.

IV. Determine Your Financial Need

To determine a student's financial need, the federal government, the state governments and the majority of universities start by reading the Free Application for Federal Student Aid (FAFSA). The FAFSA is the first step in applying for financial aid because it provides the data needed to evaluate a student's financial situation. A student's financial aid eligibility is based upon the following equation:

Financial Aid Need or Eligibility =
Cost of Attendance (COA) − Expected Family Contribution (EFC)

Although the Cost of Attendance (COA) will vary from school to school, it is defined as: "the total amount it will cost you to go to school. The COA includes tuition and fees; room and board (or a housing and food allowance for off-campus students); and allowances for books, supplies, transportation, loan fees, and dependent care. It also includes other expenses, like an allowance for the rental or purchase of a personal computer; costs related to a disability; and costs for eligible study-abroad programs."[7] The Expected Family Contribution (EFC) is calculated by the financial aid offices but is based upon a family's size, income, savings, investments, retirement savings and debt. The EFC should remain constant at each public institution within a student's home state.

Private universities look at financial need or eligibility differently than state colleges. State universities must abide by state guidelines while private colleges operate as businesses with bottom lines. As a result, private colleges do not always provide 100% demonstrated financial need aid to all students that they accept. Funding for aid at individual universities primarily comes from endowments, capital campaigns or media contracts. When a university consistently generates lucrative funding from these programs, it is typically able to offer more attractive financial aid packages to students. These circumstances have given rise to two terms when discussing admissions and financial aid; **need-blind** and **need-aware**. **Need-blind** means that the decision to admit a student to a university is solely based upon academic credentials. The need for financial aid does not play a role in admissions in any way. Ultimately, if they accept a student they will offer 100% demonstrated financial need aid. Colleges such as MIT, Harvard, Princeton and Yale are need-blind to both U.S. and international students while Stanford, Northwestern and Columbia are primarily need-blind to U.S. citizens. For a list of need-blind universities, go to www.blog.collegegreenlight.com/blog/colleges-that-meet-100-of-student-financial-need/#C17.

Need-aware means that at some point in the admissions process, a student's demonstrated need for financial aid becomes a factor in determining acceptance to that university. Typically, all applications are read once and judged on academic merit before any evaluation of financial aid is considered. Financial need is only one factor in the admissions process for private universities, but it must be addressed. A university that realizes it does not have enough funding to support a proposed class of candidates must change the mix of potential students in order to run the institution in the black. It is important to note that all universities are not either need-blind or need-aware. Many colleges will accept a student recognizing that the financial aid package they can extend will not cover all the student's costs but hope that that student can find another way to meet expenses. Alternatively, a very bright student may apply to a less competitive school in order to secure more financial aid. In order to find out a university's position on how it processes applications and distributes financial aid, students should speak to their high school college counselors, go to the university's website or contact the financial aid office directly.

To further assist a university in determining a student's financial eligibility, the institution may require a **College Scholarship Service Financial Aid Profile (CSS/PRO-FILE)**. (See Chapter #10) A CSS/PROFILE is an application distributed by the College Board that typically allows a student to apply for non-federal financial aid and scholarships at certain universities. Close to 400 institutions in the United States use the CSS/PROFILE to administer their scholarships and financial aid. Students should research each institution's specifications. For participating CSS/PROFILE subscribers, go to www.profile.collegeboard.org/profile/ppl/participatinginstitutions.aspx. In order to identify a university's position on how it processes applications and distributes financial aid, students should go to the university's website and/or contact the financial aid office directly.

V. Estimating Your Financial Need or Eligibility and Expected Family Contribution (EFC)

Estimating a student's demonstrated need for college aid and the financial contribution expected of the family is simplified by both the U.S. Department of Education and universities themselves. The Department of Education offers an online program called **FAFSA4caster** that allows you to enter information about your family's size, income, savings, investments, retirement savings and debt and calculate an **estimate** of the financial aid you can expect to receive from the federal government. The purpose of this program is to give students and families "a free, early estimate of your eligibility for federal student aid. This information helps families plan ahead for college."[8] (Remember, this might change based upon the costs and aid or scholarship funding associated with each university.) It will also calculate your EFC. (**NOTE:** The EFC should not change among home-state, public universities because it is based upon your personal financial situation, but if your financial situation changes, your EFC will change as well.) FAFSA4caster does not require you to submit any paperwork or verify your information. The purpose is for you to see how much federal aid you should expect to receive based upon you current financial status. To estimate your financial eligibility by FAFSA4caster, go to www.studentaid.ed.gov/sa/fafsa/estimate.

Many universities also offer students and parents the means to predict financial aid. The majority of colleges offer an online program called **net price calculator (NPC)**, which can be found on a university's financial aid website. Net price calculator is "a tool that allows current and prospective students, families and other consumers to estimate the net price of attending a particular college or career school."[9] Most net price calculations require information about your family's size, income, savings, investments, retirement accounts and debt. Some colleges request very specific information, such as your social security number, before you get started while others are quite flexible, allowing you to change data easily. Since the amount of information required varies by institution, the projections you receive will only be **estimates**. These estimates should, however, prove directionally accurate and provide you with a sense of the financial aid offer you might receive in the future should your student apply and be accepted to a particular university. NPC will also calculate your EFC.

Colleges that use net price calculator do not require you to submit any paperwork or verify your information in order to get an estimate. Again, the purpose is for families to see the actual cost that students should expect to pay at a specific institution based upon their current financial situations. For information about financial eligibility at an individual university, go to the financial aid section of their website and look for Net Price Calculator.

REALITY CHECK

There are many factors that impact a student's financial aid package from private universities. Besides the obvious cost of attendance, as I mentioned earlier, the availability of money typically generated from endowments, capital campaigns or media contracts will dictate how much a private university can offer students. Depending on the goals or philosophy of a university during a given year, these funds can be focused on geographical diversity, academia, engineering majors, athletics, etc. One tactic some universities have used to attract academically strong students is to offer aid in the form of grants or scholarships. Many students who want to avoid college debt or may have plans for graduate school are accepting these offers and often enroll in the university's honors programs. Typically, honors programs are more demanding, highly selective, have GPA requirements and offer students additional benefits including research opportunities and unique courses. These programs provide students with a challenging academic environment as well as an incentive to attend.

Knowing what your EFC is will assist you and your students in making some basic decisions about where they may want to focus their college search. Troy Onink, CEO of Stratagee, and Forbes made it easy for us when they published a "2016 Guide to FAFSA, CSS Profile, College Aid and Expected Family Contribution." For a ballpark estimate of your EFC, please see Exhibit #1.

EXHIBIT 1   Forbes 2017–2018 Guide To FAFSA, CSS Profile, College Aid And Expected Family Contribution

The table below can be used as a guide for your Expected Family Contribution. Its intent is to give you a simplified quick reference to EFC. The following summary will help you read and interpret the table:

"2017–2018 EFC QUICK REFERENCE TABLE FOR COLLEGE AID ELIGIBILITY

Step 1—Locate your income in the AGI column.

Step 2—Find the column at the top of the table that corresponds to the number of dependent children that you have and follow that column down to the row that corresponds with your income (AGI). The intersecting number is your estimated Federal EFC based on parental income only. The estimated EFCs in the table below do not take into account your assets, or if you make contributions to qualified retirement plans or receive any form of untaxed income. All of which will increase EFC."[10]

Color Codes
All of the EFCs are color coded to give you an idea of whether the student will qualify for need-based financial aid. The color coded EFCs in the table are based upon national average costs and your income only.

EXHIBIT 1 Forbes 2017–2018 Guide To FAFSA, CSS Profile, College Aid And Expected Family Contribution *(continued)*

2017–2018 FEDERAL EFC QUICK REFERENCE TABLE

2017-2018 Federal EFC Quick Reference Table

Number of Dependent children

AGI	1	2	3	4
$30,000	$998	$0	$0	$0
$32,500	$1,435	$582	$0	$0
$35,000	$1,871	$1,018	$0	$0
$37,500	$2,307	$1,455	$668	$0
$40,000	$2,733	$1,891	$1,103	$0
$42,500	$3,142	$2,328	$1,539	$625
$45,000	$3,074	$2,739	$1,975	$1,061
$47,500	$3,539	$3,148	$2,389	$1,498
$50,000	$4,004	$3,081	$2,808	$1,934
$52,500	$4,412	$3,545	$3,217	$2,343
$55,000	$4,951	$4,010	$3,159	$2,752
$57,500	$5,383	$4,419	$3,624	$3,161
$60,000	$6,015	$4,958	$3,972	$3,096
$62,500	$6,500	$5,391	$4,511	$3,560
$65,000	$7,244	$6,023	$5,050	$4,025
$67,500	$7,834	$6,510	$5,499	$4,437
$70,000	$8,708	$7,253	$6,131	$4,976
$72,500	$9,581	$7,846	$6,636	$5,412
$75,000	$10,455	$8,719	$7,380	$6,044
$80,000	$12,202	$10,466	$8,867	$7,277
$85,000	$13,949	$12,214	$10,615	$8,747
$90,000	$15,697	$13,961	$12,362	$10,495
$95,000	$17,219	$15,655	$14,109	$12,242
$100,000	$18,731	$17,168	$15,740	$13,989
$105,000	$20,244	$18,680	$17,252	$15,557
$110,000	$21,756	$20,192	$18,764	$17,069
$115,000	$23,268	$21,587	$20,159	$18,464
$120,000	$24,016	$22,218	$20,790	$19,095

2017-2018 Federal EFC Quick Reference Table

Number of Dependent Children

AGI	1	2	3	4
$125,000	$25,677	$24,165	$22,330	$20,635
$130,000	$27,335	$25,301	$23,874	$22,175
$135,000	$28,993	$26,959	$25,414	$23,719
$140,000	$30,651	$28,617	$26,954	$25,259
$145,000	$32,309	$30,275	$28,495	$26,800
$150,000	$33,967	$31,933	$30,035	$28,340
$155,000	$35,578	$33,544	$31,646	$29,833
$160,000	$37,180	$35,155	$33,257	$31,327
$165,000	$38,721	$36,738	$34,868	$32,760
$170,000	$40,261	$38,279	$36,432	$34,077
$175,000	$41,802	$39,819	$37,973	$35,512
$180,000	$43,342	$41,359	$39,513	$36,947
$185,000	$44,882	$42,900	$40,976	$38,381
$190,000	$46,423	$44,440	$42,410	$39,816
$195,000	$48,010	$46,028	$43,892	$41,298
$200,000	$49,598	$47,615	$45,374	$42,779
$205,000	$51,185	$49,182	$46,855	$44,261
$210,000	$52,772	$50,664	$48,337	$45,743
$215,000	$54,360	$52,145	$49,819	$47,224
$220,000	$55,947	$53,627	$51,300	$48,706
$225,000	$57,535	$55,109	$52,782	$50,188
$230,000	$59,015	$56,552	$54,226	$51,631
$235,000	$60,438	$57,975	$55,649	$53,054
$240,000	$61,861	$59,398	$57,072	$54,477
$245,000	$63,284	$60,821	$58,494	$55,900
$250,000	$64,707	$62,244	$59,917	$57,323
$275,000	$71,821	$69,359	$67,032	$64,438

© Copyright 2016. Troy Onink. All rights reserved.

*Purple and Dark Purple

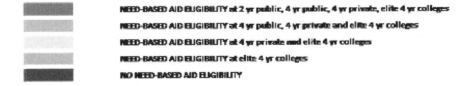

NEED-BASED AID ELIGIBILITY at 2 yr public, 4 yr public, 4 yr private, elite 4 yr colleges

NEED-BASED AID ELIGIBILITY at 4 yr public, 4 yr private and elite 4 yr colleges

NEED-BASED AID ELIGIBILITY at 4 yr private and elite 4 yr colleges

NEED-BASED AID ELIGIBILITY at elite 4 yr colleges

NO NEED-BASED AID ELIGIBILITY

This table has been reproduced in greyscale due to the printing constraints of this publication. An explanation of the color codes is depicted to the side of the graph. See the link below to view this graph in full color.

Source: Onink, Troy. 2017–2018 Guide to College Financial Aid, the FAFSA, and CSS Profile. *Forbes* 8 Jan. 2017. Web. 14 Jan. 2019. <http://www.forbes.com/sites/troyonink/2017/01/08/2017-guide-to-college-financial-aid-the-fafsa-and-css-profile/#136c41204cd4>.

federal financial aid

STEP #1

Read over the Free Application for Federal Student Aid (FAFSA) form.

STEP #2

Recognize the types of Federal Financial Aid Awards: Grants, Loans and Work-Study opportunities.

STEP #3

Identify Federal Grants including **Federal Pell Grants, Federal Supplemental Educational Opportunity Grants (FSEOG), Teacher Education Assistance for College and Higher Education (TEACH) Grants** and **Iraq and Afghanistan Service Grants**.

STEP #4

Identify Federal College Loans including **Direct Subsidized Loans, Direct Unsubsidized Loans, Direct PLUS Loans, Direct Consolidation Loans** and the **Federal Perkins Loan Program**.

STEP #5

Get to know what Federal Work-Study Programs are about.

Background

Federal Student Aid Programs were authorized under Title IV of the Higher Education Act of 1965. The Federal Student Aid Office, a division of the U.S. Department of Education, is the largest provider of financial aid in the nation, contributing more than $150 billion in federal funding to more than 15 million students a year. The Title

IV Legislative Act of 1965 authorized grants, loans and work-study funds from the federal government to eligible students enrolled in college or career schools. Eligible students may be independent or dependent. In general, an independent student is one of the following: at least 24 years old, married, a graduate or professional student, a veteran, a member of the armed forces, an orphan, a ward of the court, someone with legal dependents other than a spouse, an emancipated minor or someone who is homeless or at risk of becoming homeless. A student who does not meet any of these criteria is deemed dependent. (Go to www.studentaid.ed.gov for details about independent versus dependent student status.)

I. Free Application for Federal Student Aid (FAFSA)

The starting point for students seeking financial aid from the federal government is the Free Application for Federal Student Aid or the FAFSA. This one application enables students to apply for federal aid as well as state and college aid or scholarships. Note that individual colleges may require an additional form called the College Scholarship Service Financial Aid Profile (CSS/PROFILE). For information on the CSS/PROFILE, see Chapter #10. Here are the major components of the FAFSA:

1) It is approximately **six pages in length**.

2) It can be submitted **electronically** or via the U.S. Post Office.

3) Students and parents need to activate an **FSA ID** in order for the student to submit a FAFSA electronically. The FSA ID consists of a user- created username and password that is needed to enter and access personal data as well as to electronically sign and submit the FAFSA form. Creating the FSA ID requires a social security number, address, selection of 5 security questions, and an immediate verification that will be emailed to you. In order to complete the initiation of the FSA ID, you will need access to your email so have your iPhone or computer ready. Before you can use your FSA ID, the Social Security Administration (SSA) will verify your identity. Within 2–3 business days, you will receive an email confirming your SSA match. At this point, you will be able to use your FDA ID to file a FAFSA. To create a FSA ID, go to fsaid.ed.gov/npas/index.htm.

4) The FAFSA is **available each year on July 1**.

5) It can be **filed on or after October 1**.

6) The FAFSA **deadline** from the federal government for a fall term is typically June 30, but many **states and universities** want it sooner. Check deadlines and requirements within your individual state and for your designated college.

7) A FAFSA Application has seven steps. The following summarizes the information **required** of dependent students and their parents:

   a) Full Legal Name

   b) Address/Residence

   c) Date of birth

d) Citizenship

e) Social Security Number

f) Driver's License Number

g) Education

h) Military Service

i) Marital status

j) Number of Dependents

k) Income—Single year based upon 2 years prior

l) Savings

m) Investments

8) The application must be **signed and dated** by the dependent student and parent or by the independent student.

9) A copy of income tax forms does not have to be submitted with the application, **but colleges may request** that documentation.

10) FAFSA **information is sent to the individual colleges identified** on the application.

11) Filing a **FAFSA is free**. To complete the form online, go to www.fafsa.ed.gov.

12) A **sample FAFSA application** for July 1, 2016–June 30, 2017 is available to print in English or Spanish. Go to www.fafsa.ed.gov/fotw1819/pdf/PdfFafsa18-19.pdf.

It is extremely important that all the information in this application is accurate. Any errors that need correcting will not only delay your federal financial aid award but could also affect the amount of aid you are eligible to receive. Aid from state and any individual colleges that use the FAFSA will most likely be impacted as well. For future reference, print a copy of the application and keep it for your records.

REALITY CHECK

Gathering the information and submitting a FAFSA is not as quick and easy as you may think. Anyone I have ever spoken to about it said it took more time than they expected. If you are not sure whether you will qualify for any grants (such as two-income families that own their own homes), I would definitely recommend you take the time and make the effort to file a FAFSA anyway. Students who do not qualify for a grant may qualify for a federal or state low-interest loan. (Also, a FAFSA needs to be submitted for students to be eligible for aid or scholarships from many private university funds.) The money you and your student could potentially save in interest charges alone is worth all the trouble. The moral of this story: file your FAFSA and file it on time! The main reason eligible families don't receive aid is missed deadlines.

II. Types of Federal Financial Aid

Federal aid comes in three forms—grants, loans and work-study programs. The U.S. Department of Education offers these programs to students attending four- year colleges or universities, community colleges or career schools.

A. Grants

Grants typically do not have to be repaid. Students who file a FAFSA are automatically considered for a federal grant. Each federal grant has different eligibility requirements and is not available at every institution. Students should check to see if they qualify as potential candidates and find out about which colleges offer grants. The federal grants currently available are listed below. If you have any questions, contact your college financial aid office or go to the Federal Aid Student website at www.studentaid.ed.gov/ sa/types/grants-scholarships.

1) **Federal Pell Grants**

   a) The Federal Pell Grants are usually awarded to students with exceptional financial need.

   b) A Pell Grant is awarded to eligible **students who apply under the FAFSA.**

   c) This grant **does not have to be repaid** under most circumstances. (For exceptions, go to www.studentaid.ed.gov/sa/types/grants-scholarships#why-repay-grant.)

   d) Grants are usually **awarded only to undergraduate students** who have not earned a bachelor's or a professional degree.

   e) The **amount** awarded under the Pell Grant can change yearly. The maximum Federal Pell Grant for **July 1, 2017 to June 30, 2018 was $5,920**. The maximum Federal Pell Grant for **July 1, 2018–June 30, 2019 is $6,095.**

   f) The amount students receive from Pell Grants **depends on financial need**, the cost of attendance, their status as full-time or part-time students and whether they plan to attend school for a full academic year or not.

   g) Students may not receive these grant funds from more than **one school** at a time.

   h) "If you're **eligible** for a Federal Pell Grant, you'll receive the full amount you qualify for—each school participating in the program receives enough funds each year from the U.S. Department of Education to pay the Federal Pell Grant amounts for all its eligible students. The amount of any other student aid for which you might qualify does not affect the amount of your Federal Pell Grant."[1]

   i) "You can receive the Federal Pell Grant for no more than **12 semesters** or the equivalent (roughly six years)."[2]

   j) "Your school can **apply Federal Pell Grant funds to your school costs**, pay you directly, or combine these methods."[3] Contact the financial aid office at each university to verify payment procedures.

k) For **more information** or clarification on Federal Pell Grants, go to its website at studentaid.ed.gov/sa/types/grants-scholarships/pell.

2) **Federal Supplemental Educational Opportunity Grant (FSEOG)**

   a) This grant is **subsidized by the Federal Government** for undergraduate students who demonstrate exceptional financial need.

   b) To be considered for an FSEOG students must **file a FAFSA.**

   c) The FSEOG **does not need to be repaid.**

   d) The FSEOG program is **administered directly by the financial aid office at each participating school** and is therefore called campus-based aid. Not all schools participate. Check with your school's financial aid office to find out if it offers the FSEOG.

   e) An FSEOG **award ranges from $100 to $4,000 a year**, depending on financial need, when the application is submitted, the amount of other aid students have been given and the availability of funds at the school.

   f) Each participating **school receives a certain amount of FSEOG funds each year** from the U.S. Department of Education's office of Federal Student Aid. Once the full amount of the school's FSEOG fund has been awarded to students, no more of these grants can be given out for that year.

   g) "Each school sets its own **deadlines** for campus-based funds. You can find a school's deadline on its website or by asking someone in its financial aid office."[4]

   h) FSEOG **payment procedures** include crediting a student's account, paying the student directly or a combination of the two. FSEOG funds are distributed at least twice a year.

   i) For **more information** or clarification on FSEOG, go to studentaid.ed.gov/sa/types/grants-scholarships/fseog.

3) **Teacher Education Assistance for College and Higher Education (TEACH) Grants**

   a) "A TEACH Grant can help you **pay for college if you plan to become a teacher** in a high-need field in a low-income area."[5] ("High-need fields are bilingual education and English language acquisition, foreign language, mathematics, reading specialist, science, and special education, as well as any other field that has been identified as high-need by the federal government, a state government, or a local education agency and that is included in the annual Teacher Shortage Area national listing."[6] For TS, go to www.tsa.ed.gov/#/home/.)

   b) To be considered for a TEACH Grant, students must **file a FAFSA.**

   c) A "TEACH Grant is different from other federal student grants because it **requires you to take certain kinds of classes** in order to get the grant, and then do a certain kind of job to keep the grant from turning into a loan."[7]

   d) This program provides **grants of up to $4,000 a year** to students who are completing or plan to complete the course work needed to begin a career in education.

e) The grant requires students to "**sign a TEACH Grant Agreement to Serve** in which they agree (among other requirements) to teach in a high-need field, at an elementary school, secondary school or educational service agency that serves students from low-income families, for at least four complete academic years within eight years after completing (or ceasing enrollment in) the course of study for which they received the grant."[8]

f) "If you **do not complete your service obligation**, all TEACH Grant funds you received will be converted to a Direct Unsubsidized Loan. You must then repay this loan to the U.S. Department of Education, with interest charged from the date the TEACH Grant was disbursed (paid to you or on your behalf)."[9]

g) "The U.S. Department of Education (ED) has adopted a standardized annual certification date for all TEACH Grant recipients. This change, which begins in 2019, simplifies the annual certification requirements by having only one certification date—Oct. 31—for all Teach Grant recipients."[10]

h) Contact the financial aid office at the college where you would like to enroll in order to find out whether or not the school participates in the TEACH Grant Program. For **questions**, go to studentaid.ed.gov/sa/types/grants-scholarships/teach.

4) **Iraq and Afghanistan Service Grant**

a) "Iraq and Afghanistan Service Grants **provide money to college or career school students** to help pay their education expenses. However, Iraq and Afghanistan Service Grants have special eligibility criteria."[11]

b) To be considered for an Iraq and Afghanistan Service Grant, students must **file a FAFSA**.

c) "You may be eligible to receive the Iraq and Afghanistan Service Grant if **you are not eligible for a Federal Pell Grant** on the basis of your Expected Family Contribution **but** meet the remaining Federal Pell Grant eligibility requirements, **and** your parent or guardian was a member of the U.S. armed forces **and** died as a result of military service performed in Iraq or Afghanistan after the events of 9/11, **and** you were under 24 years old or enrolled in college at least part-time."[12]

d) "The **grant award** is **equal to** the amount of a maximum **Federal Pell Grant** for the award year but cannot exceed your cost of attendance for that award year. For the 2018–2019 award year (July 1, 2018–June 30, 2019), the maximum Federal Pell Grant award is $6,095."[13]

e) An institution can **apply Iraq and Afghanistan Service Grants to students' school costs**, pay them directly or combine these methods.

f) For more information or clarification on Iraq and Afghanistan Service Grants, go to studentaid.ed.gov/sa/types/grants-scholarships/iraq-afghanistan-service #eligibility.

B. Federal College Loans

A federal student loan is money borrowed to help pay for college expenses that must be repaid with interest. Federal loans often have low interest rates and offer flexible payment plans including income-based repayment plans and loan deferment options. Alternatively, private student loans, typically issued by a bank or a credit union, have higher fixed interest rates, require credit checks and do not offer negotiable payment plans. In order to be considered for a federal student loan, a student must file a FAFSA. **Direct Loans are generally included as part of your financial aid package.** Loan awards vary annually by program and are subject to change. The following is a summary of the federal loan opportunities:

1) **The William D. Ford Federal Direct Loan Program (Stafford Loans)**

   a) **Direct Subsidized Loans**

      1) Direct Subsidized Loans are **offered to eligible undergraduate students** who are enrolled at least half-time in a college, community college or a trade, career or technical school.

      2) To be considered for a Direct Subsidized Loan, students must **file a FAFSA.**

      3) Students **must demonstrate financial need** to help cover the costs of higher education at a college, community college and a trade, career or technical school to receive this.

      4) **The interest rate** for a Direct Subsidized Loan in the last three academic years are as follows: **2017–2018, 3.76%; 2018–2019, 5.05%.**

      5) Each **school determines the amount** students can borrow under the Direct Subsidized Loan. The loan value is based upon the cost of attendance and any other financial aid the student has received.

      6) The **loan amount varies each year** based upon other financial aid awards but typically will not exceed $3,500–$5,500 per year with a maximum loan limit of $23,000 for undergraduate studies.

      7) The **U.S. Department of Education is the lender** for these loans.

      8) Students are **not responsible for the interest** on a Direct Subsidized Loan while they are in school at least half-time, for the first six months after they leave school and during a period of deferment (a postponement of a loan payment).

      9) Payment of the loan **becomes due** after students graduate, leave school, or drop below half-time enrollment. There is a six-month grace period before they are required to begin repayment.

      10) There is a **loan fee** on all Direct Subsidized Loans that equates to a percentage of the loan amount. The percentage is subject to minor fluctuations, which is evident in the fees for the loans issued in the last three years. **October 1, 2016–October 1, 2017, 1.069%; October 1, 2017–October 1, 2018, 1.066%; October 1, 2018–October 1, 2019, 1.062%.**

11) In order to receive this loan, students are required to complete **entrance counseling which helps them understand** what it means to take out a federal student loan.

12) **Students** will be required to sign a **Master Promissory Note (MPN)**, a legal document stating that they promise to repay the loan and any accrued interest and fees to the U.S. Department of Education.

13) Direct Subsidized Loans are **applied by the school to students' school accounts** to pay for tuition, fees, room and board and other miscellaneous school charges. If any additional loan funds are left over, the school will give them to the student. All loan funds must be used by the student for educational expenses.

14) For **more information** or clarification on Direct Subsidized Loans, go to studentaid.ed.gov/sa/types/loans/subsidized-unsubsidized.

b) **Direct Unsubsidized Loans**

1) Direct Unsubsidized Loans are **made to eligible undergraduate**, graduate and professional students who are enrolled at least half-time in an accredited institution.

2) To be considered for this loan, students must **file a FAFSA**.

3) **Undergraduate students** who received a Direct Unsubsidized Loan over the past three years were charged the following rates: 2016–2017, 3.76%; 2017–2018, 4.45%; 2018–2019, 6.6%.

4) Each **school determines the amount** students can borrow. The loan value will be based upon the cost of attendance and any other financial aid the students have received.

5) The **loan amount can vary** each year based upon other financial aid awards, grade level and dependency status, but generally the loan amount for undergraduate students **will range from $5,500–$7,500 per year** with a maximum loan amount of $31,000 for dependent students. For independent students, the range is **$9,500–$12,500 per year** with a maximum loan amount of $57,500.

6) The U.S. Department of Education is the lender for these loans.

7) **Students are responsible for the interest** on a Direct Unsubsidized Loan while in school, during any grace periods and deferment periods. If interest payments are not made while students are in school, the interest will accumulate and it will be added to the principal amount of the loan.

8) **Repayment** of the Direct Unsubsidized Loan plus interest is due after students graduate, leave school or drop below half-time enrollment. There is a six-month grace period before students are required to begin repayment.

9) There is a **loan fee** on all Direct Unsubsidized Loans, which equates to a percentage of the loan amount and is proportionally deducted from

each loan disbursement. The percentage is subject to minor fluctuations, which is evident in the fees for the loans issued in the last three years. **October 1, 2016–October 1, 2017, 1.069%; October 1, 2017–October 1, 2018, 1.066%; October 1, 2018–October 1, 2019, 1.062%.**

10) In order to receive this loan, students are required to complete **entrance counseling which helps them understand** what it means to take out a federal student loan.

11) Students are required to **sign a Master Promissory Note** (MPN), a legal document stating that they promise to repay the loan and any accrued interest and fees to the U.S. Department of Education.

12) Direct Unsubsidized Loans are **applied by the school to students' school accounts** to pay for tuition, fees, room and board and other miscellaneous school charges. If any additional loan funds remain, the school will give them to the student.

13) For **more information** or clarification on Direct Unsubsidized Loans, go to studentaid.ed.gov/sa/types/loans/subsidized-unsubsidized .

REALITY CHECK

The vast majority of college-bound students are eligible to receive some Federal Direct Student loans regardless of their parents' incomes. Whether these loans will be subsidized or unsubsidized is contingent upon the family's financial situation. Over four years, the federal unsubsidized student loans currently offered to students increase from $9,500 freshman year to $10,500 sophomore year and top off at $12,500 for both junior and senior years. Again, these loans are guaranteed by the federal government and offer some of the best terms you and your student will find anywhere. If you know you need help to finance college, this is a good place to start.

c) **Direct PLUS Loans**

1) Direct PLUS Loans are **made to graduate** or professional students and **parents of dependent undergraduate students** to help pay for educational expenses not covered by other financial aid.

2) To be **eligible** for a Direct PLUS Loan, a student must be enrolled at least half-time in an accredited program that will lead to a certificate or degree. The graduate, professional student or child of the parent who is borrowing must meet the general eligibility requirements for federal student aid.

3) To be considered for this loan, students or their parents must **file a FAFSA**.

4) Before a Direct PLUS Loan is issued, **a credit check will be run** on the borrower. The borrower cannot have a negative credit history in order to receive a Direct PLUS Loan.

5) The interest rate for Direct PLUS Loans disbursed over the last three years are as follows: **July 1, 2016–July 1, 2017, 6.31%; July 1, 2017–July 1, 2018, 7.00%; July 1, 2018–July 1, 2019, 7.6%.**

6) **Loan amounts vary by institution.** There are no minimum amounts that can be borrowed but the maximum amount of a Direct PLUS Loan cannot exceed the cost of attendance minus any other financial aid received.

7) The **U.S. Department of Education is the lender** for Direct PLUS Loans and the loan amount is owed to it.

8) Graduate students or parents of the dependent undergraduates (the borrowers) are **responsible for the interest** on these loans while the students are in school, during any grace periods and deferment periods. If a request is made to defer the interest payments while students are attending school, the interest will accumulate and it will be added to the principal amount of the loan. Deferments are available to borrowers if students are enrolled at least half-time.

9) **Repayment** of the Direct PLUS Loan, including accumulated interest, is due after students graduate, leave school or drop below half-time enrollment. Graduate students or parents of dependent students have a six-month grace period before they are required to begin repayment.

10) There is a **loan fee** on all Direct PLUS Loans, which equates to a percentage of the loan amount and is proportionally deducted from each loan disbursement. The percentage is subject to fluctuations, which is evident in the fees for the loans issued in the last three years: **October 1, 2016–October 1, 2017, 4.276%; October 1, 2017–October 1, 2018, 4.264%; October 1, 2018–October 1, 2019, 4.248%.**

11) In order to receive a Direct PLUS Loan, the borrowers, graduate students, professional students or parents are required to sign a **Master Promissory Note** (MPN), a legal document stating that the borrowers promise to repay the loan and any accrued interest and fees to the U.S. Department of Education.

12) Graduate or professional students are also required to complete **entrance counseling**, which helps them understand what it means to take out a federal student loan.

13) Direct PLUS Loans **are applied by the school to students' school accounts** to pay for tuition, fees, room and board, and other miscellaneous school charges. If any additional loan funds remain, the school will return them to the students.

14) If a parent borrower is unable to secure a PLUS loan, the student may qualify for an additional unsubsidized loan. The student should contact the college financial aid office.

15) For **more information** or clarification on Direct PLUS Loans, go to studentaid.ed.gov/sa/types/loans/plus.

REALITY CHECK

When I asked my savvy, competent niece, who graduated from the University of Alabama, what she wished she knew about financial aid, she said, "I wish I knew more about Parent/Direct PLUS loans." A friend had told her about them when she was a senior in college trying to figure out how she was going to finance her last semester. Unfortunately, it was too late for her to explore the PLUS loan option and she ultimately secured a loan from a private lender, which very likely, cost her more to acquire.

Tips for Parent Plus Loans

Tip #1 *"If a parent borrower is unable to obtain a PLUS loan, the undergraduate dependent student may be eligible for additional unsubsidized loans. The student should contact the school's financial aid office for more information."*[14]

Tip #2 *"The US Department of Education offers two main types of discounts on Direct Loans:*

- *0.25% interest rate reduction for auto-debit*

- *1.5% rebate at the time of disbursement, retained by making the first 12 payments on time."*[15]

2) **Direct Consolidation Loans**

a) Direct Consolidation Loans are **administered by the U.S. Department of Education**.

b) These loans allow students to **combine all of their eligible federal student loans into a single loan** with a single loan servicer.

c) These loans simplify repayment with one bill per month.

d) There is no application fee with Direct Consolidation Loans.

e) Most federal student loans are **eligible** for consolidation.

f) Students are generally **eligible** for a Direct Consolidation Loan **after they graduate**, leave school or drop below half-time enrollment.

g) A Direct Consolidation Loan may give students access to **alternative repayment plans** and extend the terms of repayment up to 30 years.

h) A consolidation of loans may also **affect the interest rate, principal rebates or cancellation benefits on an individual loan.** This can significantly impact the cost of repaying those loans. Students should be aware of the positive and negative financial implications before consolidating federal student loans.

i) "A Direct Consolidation Loan has a **fixed interest rate** for the life of the loan. The fixed rate is based on the weighted average of the interest rates on the loans being consolidated, rounded up to the nearest one-eighth of 1%. There is no cap on the interest rate of a Direct Consolidation Loan."[16]

j) Once your loans have been **combined** into a Direct Consolidation Loan, they **cannot be removed**.

k) **Repayment** of a Direct Consolidation Loan can begin up to 60 days after the loan is disbursed depending upon the individual's loans and circumstances.

l) **To apply** for a Direct Consolidation Loan, students need to complete an electronic or paper application from the StudentLoans.gov website. To access this application, students need to have a FSA ID number. (See Federal Student Aid above)

m) For **more information** or questions on Direct Consolidation Loans, contact the Loan Consolidation Information Call Center at 1-800-557-7392.

REALITY CHECK

Consolidating loans from the federal government or even a private lender sounds like such a great idea, especially when you see the commercials from private lenders that tell you to take a vacation with the money you are saving. Federal loan consolidation may be more reasonable than a private consolidation, but do not be fooled by promotions like this. Recognize that, ultimately, students will be paying even more for that college education than it actually costs! Any low interests loans your student has will be averaged up and combined with higher interest ones. Yes, loan consolidation makes people's lives a lot easier to manage and may enable them to handle financial commitments, but consolidation "can result in loss of some benefits."[17] This means that consolidation can significantly impact the cost of repaying those loans, especially if you extend the repayment period. Beware. Any lender who offers you or your student the opportunity to consolidate college loans is doing so because they will profit from it. Students are their new target market.

3) **Federal Perkins Loan Program (Perkins Loan)**

   a) Federal Perkins Loans were offered to undergraduate and graduate students with **exceptional financial need**.

   b) Federal Perkins loans are no longer available for any students. "Under federal law, the authority for schools to make new Perkins Loans ended on Sept. 30, 2017."[18] For more information, go to www.studentaid.ed.gov/sa/types/loans/perkins.

C. Work-Study

The federal work-study program is financial aid that requires students to work for funding which helps cover the cost of college or living expenses. This program supports community service work or work that may be related to students' fields of study. Here are the leading factors associated with Federal Work Study programs:

1) These programs provide **part–time employment**.

2) They are awarded to **undergraduate and graduate students**.

3) Federal Work-Study is **available to part-time and full-time students**.

4) To be considered for Federal Work Study, students or parents must **file a FAFSA**.

5) Candidates must **demonstrate financial need**.

6) Federal Work Study programs **pay minimum wage or better** depending upon the work and grade level of the student. Undergraduate students are paid by the hour while graduate students may be paid a salary or by the hour.

7) Federal Work-Study hours are absolute. Students' **hours and pay cannot exceed** the work-study **award**.

8) **Students are paid directly** at least once a month.

9) Federal Work-Study jobs can be **located on or off campus**, depending upon the individual university.

10) These jobs may be associated with the school, a nonprofit or public agency or a specific course of study. **Employment opportunities vary by institution**.

11) The participating school oversees the Federal Work-Study program.

12) Colleges that participate in the program award jobs on **a first come, first served basis**.

13) **All institutions do NOT have Federal Work-Study programs.** Please contact the respective college to see if this program is offered.

REALITY CHECK

If you take one recommendation away from this chapter, **I hope it is to file both a FAFSA and a CSS/Profile as early as possible!** *I recognize that there is an enormous amount of information and many deadlines to deal with, especially when you are simultaneously guiding your students through this college process, but if you can think about what you need on the financial aid front early, it will make your life so much easier in the long run. Given the fact that timing is important, here is a schedule you can follow for financial aid.*

Financial Aid Suggested Time Line

Summer before Senior Year

JULY AND AUGUST

Step #1   Activate an **FSA ID.** The FSA ID consists of a user- created username and password that is needed to enter and access personal data as well as to electronically sign and submit the FAFSA form. To create a FSA ID, go to fsaid.ed.gov/npas/index.htm.

Step #2   Review the FAFSA and CSS/PROFILE (Chapter #10) online. For FAFSA, go to fafsa.ed.gov. For the CSS/Profile, go to cssprofile.collegeboard.org.

Step #3   Attend a college financial aid session while visiting schools with your students. Also look for any financial aid seminars offered by your child's high school, within your local community, online, though universities or other private sources.

Fall of Senior Year

SEPTEMBER

Step #4   Gather pertinent documents needed to fill out the FAFSA. These include: social security number, driver's license number, W-2 forms and other records of taxed and untaxed income, bank statements on savings and investments and information about education and military service. *(Note: Financial documents needed are from a single year but are based upon two years prior.)*

Step #5   Print a copy of the FAFSA from fafsa.ed.gov/fotw1819/pdf/PdfFafsa18-19.pdf.

Step #6   Set aside plenty of time to fill out the FAFSA.

Step #7   Give yourself a deadline for completing the FAFSA based upon the college requirements. It can be filed on or after October 1.

Step #8   Gather additional documents needed to fill out the CSS/PROFILE.

Step #9   Set aside plenty of time to fill out the CSS/PROFILE. It can be filled out online and saved for further edits and completion.

Step #10 Give yourself a deadline for completing the CSS/PROFILE based upon the college deadlines. It can be filed as earlier as October 1 in order for students to be considered for preliminary financial aid from an early acceptance program.

OCTOBER

Step #11 On October 1, file the FAFSA online at www.FAFSA.ed.gov.

Step #12 Receive your Expected Family Contribution (EFC) that is calculated from the data reported on your FAFSA.

Step #13 Receive your Student Aid Report (SAR). The SAR will let you make corrections, note changes in financial circumstances or include additional colleges where you would like your information sent.

Step #14 Print a copy of your FAFSA and file it for your records.

Step #15 File your CSS/PROFILE application on the College Board Website by going to student.collegeboard.org/css-financial-aid-profile. There is a $25 fee for the first profile sent and $16 for each additional one.

Step #16 Receive a Data Confirmation Report from CSS/PROFILE. Any corrections that need to be made must be reported and submitted directly to each institution's financial aid office.

Step #17 Print a copy of your CSS/PROFILE and file it for your records

OCTOBER/NOVEMBER

Step #18 Continue to review financial aid options by viewing webinars offered by colleges or third party companies. Also, attend any college financial aid seminars that you have learned about through your high school, your community or the universities your teen is interested in attending.

December

Step #19 Look for preliminary Financial Aid awards to become available for students who applied early acceptance to college and whose parents filed the FAFSA, the CSS/PROFILE or the individual university's financial aid forms.

Winter of Senior Year

JANUARY–APRIL

Step #20 Students should expect to receive Financial Aid Awards from each college they applied to. Award letters are distributed based upon how the application was submitted—ED, EA or RD.

Spring of Senior Year

MAY 1

Step #21 Students need to accept, deny or appeal the financial aid offers they have been given.

Summer of Rising College Freshman

JUNE–AUGUST

Step #22   College tuition bills are sent out.

CHAPTER 10

state, college and private financial aid

STEP #1

Identify state financial aid opportunities and requirements.

STEP #2

Identify whether Institutional financial aid is need based or merit based and if the College Scholarship Service Financial Aid Profile (CSS/PROFILE) form is required.

STEP #3

Identify private and nonprofit college scholarships and aid funded by independent organizations including community leagues, civic groups, Rotary and Kiwanis clubs, local high schools, businesses, family foundations and even some national associations. Beware of scams with college scholarship search engines.

STEP #4

Identify private and nonprofit college loans from financial institutions such as banks or credit unions to fill in the gaps of tuition costs but remember, private loans are not guaranteed, require credit checks, have higher interest rates than state or federal loans, are not flexible and accrue interest.

STEP #5

Decipher private college aid by recognizing that colleges that disburse financial aid on a need basis will not necessarily provide enough funding for students to actually attend the university, and students with two working parents will struggle to finance tuition at most universities.

STEP #6

Break the financial aid myth by being aware that universities that provide need-based financial aid may offer grants to students they are pursuing for academics or athletics and universities that do not offer sports scholarships may offer grants to students they are pursuing for academics and athletics.

STEP #7

Explore other options to help finance a college education.

I. State Financial Aid

Almost every state offers some form of financial aid for its residents to attend college. It can come in the form of grants, scholarships, tuition waivers, loans or work-study programs. Many states offer numerous financial aid options. The vast majority of states restrict eligibility to residents who are attending a university within the state, but that does not always hold true. Some offer residents the option to attend a college in a different state without paying the out-of–state tuition. This arrangement generally falls under the tuition exchange or reciprocity program.

Since each state varies in its programs, practices, deadlines and procedures for receiving financial aid, it is best to check with yours to clarify questions. Most states have a department of education or regency board that administers these aid programs. I would start the process by contacting the state's office of financial aid. The U.S. Department of Education provides an Education Resource Organization Directory of the offices of Student Financial Assistance by state. The list provides the name, address, phone number and website for each state's financial aid office. It can be found at www2.ed.gov/about/contacts/state/.

Additionally, there is a philanthropic agency in Washington D.C. called the National Association of Student Financial Aid Admissions (NAFSAA) whose vision is to shape the "future by promoting student access in higher education."[1] Its mission is to provide "professional development and services for financial aid administrators; advocates for public policies that increase student access and success; serves as a forum on student financial aid issues, and is committed to diversity throughout all activities."[2] NASFAA has six regional associations that work closely with state associations by advocating for and serving students in their communities. NAFSAA provides information and links to financial aid and scholarships for all 50 states as well as the District of Columbia, Puerto Rico, the U.S. Virgin Islands, the Pacific Islands and Guam. Their website (www.nasfaa.org/State_Financial_Aid_Programs) identifies state-funded financial aid programs for students. This website can also link students to information about the State and Region College Tuition Discounts or tuition exchange programs that may exist among states. For more information about tuition reciprocity, go to NAFSAA's website at www.nasfaa.org/State_Regional_Tuition_Exchanges.

As students explore state financial aid opportunities, it is important to remember the following:

1) Most states offer some form of financial aid for undergraduate students.

2) Each state offers different forms of financial aid.

3) The amount and type of aid students are awarded may depend upon financial need.

4) Most states require a FAFSA for students to be considered for financial aid.

5) A state may require additional financial aid forms besides the FAFSA.

6) Each state may have different deadlines for financial aid forms.

7) A state may offer grants, scholarships, tuition waivers, tuition reciprocity, loans, work-study programs or a combination of these.

8) A state's enrollment requirements for students vary.

9) It is absolutely necessary for students to check with their state's financial aid office or website to ensure they are meeting the requirements.

10) Students can find out about the department that handles financial aid in their state by going to the U.S. Department of Education Resource Directory at www2.ed.gov/about/contacts/state/.

11) Students can explore the information about their state's financial aid opportunities by visiting the National Association of Student Financial Aid Admissions (NAFSAA) website at www.nasfaa.org.

REALITY CHECK

A family friend attended a state college in the South and worked independently to support himself through four years of schooling. He rented housing off campus and was committed to a year-long lease. During his senior year, he learned from friends that had he stayed and worked summers in this state, he might have qualified as a resident. If so, his tuition could have been discounted. Additionally, he may have been better served if he had looked into the availability of a tuition exchange or reciprocity program before he applied to college. As detailed above, this program, offered in some states, enables students to attend a college in a different state without paying a higher out-of-state tuition.

II. Institutional Financial Aid and Grants

Financial aid from an individual institution can be offered in many forms such as grants, scholarships or loans. The two factors often used to determine how much aid a student receives are need and merit. **Need-based** aid is given to any student who demonstrates a lack of financial resources to pay for college tuition. A **merit-based** package is awarded to any student who excels in an area such as music, athletics or academics. Also, merit-based aid can be given to students who are pursuing a career in an area that will benefit the community or the country such as education, science, math or engineering.

As was mentioned earlier, need-based scholarships or financial aid from an individual college can be a part of a federal program. In this instance, the university makes an Institution Capital Contribution (ICC) and the government makes a Federal Government Capital Contribution (FCC) to subsidize the loan. As the loans are repaid, the funds collected are then redistributed to students who demonstrate exceptional financial need. Many universities also offer student aid that is funded through its own financial resources. These scholarships may be subsidized by endowments, alumni or even sports contracts. The amount of aid available really depends upon the university's financial constraints in a given year as well as the philosophy it tries to model. To be considered for need-based financial aid, some colleges require an additional form or a **CSS Financial Aid Profile** to be filed. (See below) To ensure they are meeting all the application requirements, students should check with each university's website and/or financial aid office.

Merit-based scholarships or grants are given to students for noteworthy skills. They often are awards that recognize and reward specific talents and entice students to attend. Students may automatically qualify for such an award when they file their college application or the FAFSA, but, generally, additional forms may be required. Students interested in exploring what merit-based scholarships or grants are available at a particular university should go to the financial aid section of the school's website to view the list of these awards. **Sports scholarships,** which are available at DI and DII schools, are negotiated by the athletes, the coaches, the athletic department, the admissions office and/or the financial aid office. As I mentioned earlier in the book, it is essential for athletes to recognize that a verbal commitment is not necessarily binding. An offer is technically not a contract until it is in writing. As for **academic scholarships,** they may be offered based solely upon the candidates' superior SAT/ACT scores and/or outstanding high school transcripts. These scholarships are usually extended as part of students' admissions packages and/or financial aid packages before they have committed to that university. Academic scholarships are often used to entice students to attend. Each university has its own focus when it comes to merit-based scholarships, so students should research what schools offer scholarships for their particular talents. A college counselor should be able to provide direction. These academic scholarships are often established in honor of an alumna or alumnus, are service oriented or associated with a field of study and range from partial to full tuition awards that are renewable for one to five years depending on the program, students' grade point averages or majors. Even though applying for any scholarship can be a hassle, the potential financial benefits far surpass the time spent completing the applications.

For students to be considered for some college scholarships, many institutions require the College Scholarship Service Financial Aid Profile, **CSS/PROFILE**. (See below.) The majority of affiliated institutions require it for need-based financial aid and scholarships, but it appears that some universities also require it for merit scholarships. Since close to 400 institutions in the United States use the CSS/PROFILE to administer their scholarships and financial aid, students should research each institution they apply to in order to determine its specifications. For a current list of colleges utilizing the CSS/PROFILE, go to profile.collegeboard.org/profile/ppi/participatingInstitutions.aspx.

The following is just a sampling of the scholarship requirements associated with a few of the universities that are part of the CSS/PROFILE:

1) **Carnegie Mellon University, Pittsburgh, PA**—The Carnegie Scholarship is awarded to academically and artistically talented middle income students who qualify for little to no need-based financial aid. Additional scholarships are available based upon merit and need but "'the CSS profile is required for institutional financial aid programs."[3]

2) **Washington University, St. Louis, MO**—Washington University requires a student applying for financial aid to file "a FAFSA, a CSS Profile or a WU Family Financial Profile and a non custodian Parent's Statement if parents are divorced, separated or never married."[4] Distribution of Financial aid from the college is need-based. Alternatively, Washington University's merit scholarship programs offer aid based on academic achievement.

3) **Stanford University, CA**—"All university scholarship funds are awarded on the basis of financial need as determined by information provided on the CSS/PRO-FILE. We determine your individual scholarship eligibility by subtracting the amount we expect you and your parents to contribute toward your costs and other federal and state grant funds from the total student budget."[5]

REALITY CHECK

University funds for financial aid are limited and often sourced from endowments, alumni and occasionally from media contracts. The earlier students submit their applications and financial aid forms, the more likely it is they will receive aid given that funds are often distributed on a first come, first served basis. While certain federal loans are available to all students, no matter when they submit the FAFSA, the funds in university aid programs are limited. It is also important to understand that universities that distribute aid based upon demonstrated financial need don't necessarily provide students with all the funding they need to attend that college. Additionally, university loans tend to have higher interest rates than even some private loans because the students they are lending to usually have no established credit. If your students are offered a university loan to finance college, you should look around and evaluate your options. You may be able to save a significant amount of money in interest rates from another source.

There is often confusion associated with universities that distribute financial aid based upon need. You should be aware that universities that provide need-based financial aid may offer grants to students it is pursuing for academics or athletics who do not meet the financial requirements in order to entice them to attend. Additionally, there may be a misperception that exists with colleges that do not offer sports scholarships. Some of them may offer grants to students they are pursuing for academics and athletics in order to lure them into attending. Grants are financial awards to be used for college tuition, room, board, etc., that are not paid back.

College Scholarship Service Financial Aid Profile (CSS/PROFILE)

The CSS/PROFILE is an application distributed by the College Board that allows students to apply for non-federal financial aid and scholarships. As I mentioned earlier, there are close to 400 institutions in the United States that utilize the CSS/PROFILE in some capacity. Typically, CSS/PROFILE colleges are selective, private universities, including the Ivies, but there are a few notable state college exceptions. The CSS/PROFILE enables an institution to evaluate an Estimated Family Contribution (EFC) based upon its own criteria. Variables such as a student's assets or a parent's home equity may be treated differently at a specific institution than they are under federal financial aid guidelines. As a result, the financial aid calculations for a student's EFC may differ under FAFSA versus the CSS/PROFILE. The following summarizes the key factors associated with the CSS/PROFILE application:

1) The **College Board is the provider and administrator of the CSS/PROFILE**. Universities contract with the College Board to collect and process a student's personal and financial information utilizing the CSS/PROFILE application.

2) A CSS/PROFILE application is utilized at U.S. institutions to assist in **determining non-federal financial aid** including institutional grants, work-study programs and scholarships.

3) A CSS/PROFILE application is **accepted by** close to **400 institutions** across the United States. For a current list of colleges, go to profileonline.collegeboard.org/ppi/participatingInstitutions.aspx.

4) **One** comprehensive CSS/PROFILE **application allows a student to apply to any of the affiliated universities** simultaneously.

5) The CSS/PROFILE application is more comprehensive than the FAFSA. It **requires additional financial information.**

6) To initiate a CSS/PROFILE application, students must **create a CSS/PROFILE account.**

7) To create an account, students should utilize the same **usernames and passwords** they employed on the College Board Website for SAT, PSAT/NMSQT or AP exam registration.

8) **To access** the CSS/PROFILE application, go the College Board website at cssprofile.collegeboard.org.

9) A CSS/PROFILE **application can be saved**. It does not need to be completed in one sitting.

10) Only **one person should be signed in** to a student's account at a time.

11) The College Board provides **online help** for the application process.

12) The **initial application fee** for the CSS/PROFILE, which includes one college or program report, is **$25 with each additional report costing $16**. Fee waivers are available and automatically granted upon completion of the profile.

13) The information on a student's CSS/PROFILE is **processed and reported** to the institutions **immediately** upon payment of the application fee.

14) Once a CSS/PROFILE is processed, you cannot change your answers electronically. Changes must be reported and submitted directly to each institution's financial aid office via fax, email or snail mail.

15) A parent or student may be **notified that additional tax information or financial documents are required under the** Institutional Documentation Service (IDOC) on the "Dashboard." A parent or student may be notified at Registration Confirmation or at Submittal Acknowledgment that those documents are needed to complete the application.

16) **Divorced or separated parents** may be required to fill out an additional form called the Noncustodial PROFILE (NCP). A parent or student may be notified at Registration Confirmation or at Submittal Acknowledgment that additional documents are needed to complete the application For more information, go to css.collegeboard.org.

17) The CSS/PROFILE can be **filed starting October 1.**

18) The **deadline** for filing the CSS/PROFILE **is unique to each university**. Please check with each institution for definitive deadlines.

REALITY CHECK

Many private and several public universities require students to fill out a CSS/PROFILE to be considered for financial aid. The CSS/PROFILE, which can be upwards of 20+ pages, will take longer to fill out than the FAFSA because, as I mentioned above, not only does it require more detailed information, but also it often calls for additional supporting financial documentation. Anyone I have ever spoken to who filed a CSS/ PROFILE said that it is time consuming and basically, a pain in the neck. To further exacerbate the process, the forms can change each year. I recommend starting early.

One reason the CSS/PROFILE **(and now, the FAFSA)** *may be submitted as early as October 1 is related to early decision(ED) and early action (EA) applications. Since ED and EA applications are filed in October and November and students receive notifications in December, submission of the CSS/PROFILE in the fall will give these students an early indication of their financial aid packages. If a student applies ED and is accepted but the financial aid package the school offers won't sufficiently fund all the costs of attending and the family can prove extreme hardship, then that student MAY be released from the otherwise binding contract. Since policies on ED and financial aid differ by school, students should check with the university before they apply.*

Even if your students are not applying ED to a university, it is still in their best interests to file the CSS/PROFILE early. (October or November) Remember university funds for financial aid are fixed. The earlier your students apply the better the package they will receive. Ron Vachon, a Registered Financial Planner in Holbrook, MA, advises clients to start gathering the information for the CSS/PROFILE as early as August or September in order to file it in October or November.

III. Private and Nonprofit College

A. Scholarships and Aid

Private and nonprofit college scholarships and aid are often funded by independent organizations that are not affiliated with any university. These organizations usually include community leagues, civic groups, Rotary and Kiwanis clubs, local high schools, businesses, family foundations and even some national associations. Many of these scholarships are merit based and require their own forms to be completed. (For scholarships based on financial need, some funding sources accept the FAFSA as financial verification while other nationally, recognized foundations might require the CSS/PROFILE.) Although these scholarships make up a very small portion of total college aid awarded to students each year, they can ultimately help defray the skyrocketing costs of higher education. Students must report any private scholarships to the university. If students have filed a FAFSA and been awarded financial aid, any private scholarships received may affect their federal, state or institutional aid. (If a scholarship exceeds the total cost of attending a school, the university will usually start by reducing loans and work-study benefits before touching any grants.) Pursuing private scholarships for college tuition can ultimately be a very rewarding experience, but students should recognize that it is also hard work and can be a very time consuming process.

The following are some strategies to explore when seeking private scholarships:

1) Students should start locally to uncover what scholarships are readily available. Your local library and high school college counselors may be connected to community and civic groups that offer scholarships.

2) High school counselors may also be knowledgeable about scholarships available at the universities the student is interested in.

3) Students should check with their local state representatives to find out if any state scholarships are available.

4) Students should look to family members and friends who might be affiliated with unions, churches, veterans associations, civic clubs, etc., in case they could be sources of revenue.

5) Students should research funding opportunities by going directly to a college's financial aid website and locating merit-based scholarships.

As a last resort, students can research the availability of scholarships through a college scholarship search engine. Since there are well over a million of these, students should be careful and selective about accessing a credible one. FAFSA suggests that a safe college scholarship search engine is free of charge, poses no risks for identity theft and allows users to report any suspected fraud. For more specific information, go to www.studentaid.ed.gov/types/scams.

Deciding which college scholarship search engine to use probably comes down to personal taste, patience and perseverance since many of them have not proven to be extraordinarily helpful to students in finding scholarship matches. It is important to note that many of these scholarship search engines do attempt to connect students with potential college scholarships but various news outlets have described their ability to do this as "mediocre at best."[6] The following is a list, not a ranking, of some of college scholarship search engines referenced in articles appearing in *Forbes Magazine* as well as on the FAFSA and NASFFA websites:

a) The College Board (bigfuture.collegeboard.org/scholarship-search)

b) Fastweb.com

c) Scholarships.com

d) U.S. Department of Labor (careeronestop.org/toolkit/training/find/scholarships)

e) Cappex.com

REALITY CHECK

Local scholarships from Kiwanis clubs or civic groups are considered untapped resources by some college advisors. Many people mistakenly believe that you need to be a member of the group in order to qualify for a scholarship, but, typically, this is not true. With minimal effort, my resourceful, determined niece was able to secure several local scholarships from the Rotary club, sports affiliated groups and memorial funds. Some of the scholarships were only offered to graduating high school seniors, while others were applicable to any full-time undergraduates. The awards ranged from $250 to $2000 and most required her to re-apply each year. Finding these scholarships takes some work and requires students to ask around. Remember that your neighborhood libraries, high school guidance counselors, local representatives and family members are the best sources for information on scholarship opportunities.

B. Loans

Loans from private financial institutions such as banks or credit unions are often utilized by students and parents to fill in the gap that exists between the cost of college and any financial aid and scholarship awards they have been given. Some of the financial institutions that underwrite these college loans are: Sallie Mae/Navient, JP Morgan Chase, Wells Fargo, Citizens Bank, AAA and ACS Education Service. Private college loans are typically characterized by the following:

1)   They are not guaranteed.

2)   They always require credit checks.

3)   The terms and interest rates of private loans vary by lender.

4)   Private loan interest rates are often impacted by the credit history of the borrower.

5)   Private loan terms will be less attractive than the terms offered by any state or federal program.

6)   There is little to no payment flexibility.

7)   Private loans begin to accrue interest as soon as the loan is disbursed even if the payments are not required until an agreed upon date in the future.

Federal and private college loans have risen to an all-time high. According to the Federal Reserve, student debt now equates to $1.6 trillion. "New York University's Constantine Yannelis and [Adam Looney] find that the share of students graduating with more than $50,000 in student debt has more than tripled since 2000, increasing from 5 percent of borrowers in 2000 to 17 percent of student borrowers in 2014. That group now holds the majority of outstanding student debt owed to the government—about $790 billion."[7] As students take on more debt to attend public and private universities, they also take on more personal financial risk. Many believe that this mounting debt could jeopardize the economy and negatively impact the future of a whole generation of young Americans. The director of the Consumer Financial Protection Bureau (CFPB) has likened the college debt situation to the recent sub-prime mortgage crisis in the U.S. As I wrote in an earlier chapter, one factor that may have led us to this situation is the ease of access to many federal college loans, and the availability of funding has also enabled universities to increase tuition and fees without impacting enrollment. Another indicator is the debt parents and grandparents have taken on to pay for students' education.

Again, how much debt you and your students can and should incur to attend a university is a personal decision. Recognize that even Federal Loan Servicers like Sallie Mae/Navient, Performant Financial and ECMC Group are running businesses: they want and need to make money. The question you and your students should ask is, "How much debt is reasonable to take on throughout a college career?" (**NOTE:** Federal loan servers may also underwrite private student loans. Sallie Mae recently moved its federal loan services to a separate company called Navient while keeping the Sallie Mae entity for private loan services.)

Many men and women are managing their college debts but some are struggling to make the monthly payments. In 2013, seven in 10 (69%) graduating seniors at public and private nonprofit colleges had student loans. According to Forbes, "the average student in the Class of 2016 has $37,172 in student loan debt."[8] This debt translates into payments of a little more than $428 per month over the standard 10-year repayment plan at an interest rate of 6.8%, according to an online repayment calculator. Should lenders be held more accountable or their practices looked at more closely on the private and federal levels? Will lenders' practices be evaluated and changed in any way? I highly encourage students and their parents to educate themselves as much as possible about the implications of owing a lot of money for a college education.

REALITY CHECK

Applying for college financial aid can be daunting, but as I said before, completely worth the effort. Evaluating the big picture of how much will be owed each month and how much students will need to earn after college in order to repay loans is important. I would suggest you not only broach the subject with your students before they ever step foot in a college dorm room but you repeatedly remind them of the implications of student debt. They need to know what they are getting into and make it worth the huge financial investment it is. A big question to ask here is public versus private. In my opinion, the amount of debt a student can incur when attending a private university can far exceed the average $37,172 in loans that was noted preciously. The fact is that a private college education can cost as much as $20,000–$30,000 more per year than a public college.

Among my own small pool of family candidates, we have had athletes and scholars who have come from both public and private high schools. Their hard-working, dedicated parents have careers in business, nursing, law enforcement, engineering, construction, electrical, real estate, accounting, printing, etc. The financial aid process for each family has been different. So I asked the parents and the students in the families what they wish they had known about the financial aid process. Their responses were many and varied. I leave you with their thoughts as well as some options to explore as you consider how to finance your students' college educations.

I Wish I Had Known . . .

. . . **everyone** should **file a FAFSA** . . . as early as October 1.

. . . we might have been **eligible for some low-interest** loans from the federal or state government if I had filed a FAFSA.

. . . most private universities **require a CSS/PROFILE** or their own forms to be considered for financial aid.

. . . the **earlier you file a FAFSA or CSS/PROFILE the better.** Universities have a fixed amount of aid and scholarships as well as the discretion to distribute it.

. . . to **check** that I was interested in the **work-study program** when I filled out the FAFSA.

. . . FAFSA **does not** take into **account any high school private tuition costs** as an expense.

. . . the **definition of demonstrated financial need** for full-time is **different** at any given university.

. . . to recognize the positive impact geography can play on financial aid and scholarships.

. . . to recognize the cost implications of a state versus private college.

. . . you may **qualify** for more **financial assistance** at a **private, prestigious** university than you do at a **state college** because of endowments.

. . . some universities, such as Indiana University, identify on their websites merit awards associated with GPA and standardized testing scores.

. . . to compare college aid and merit packages by DOing the MATH for four years of schooling.

. . . I would have **more debt** than I expected.

. . . private loan interest rates are based upon the credit history of the parents or the co-signer.

. . . what my monthly payments would be for all of my loans before I signed for them.

. . . **financial aid award letters** from individual colleges are sent to the **students** with the acceptance letter or shortly thereafter.

I Wish I Had Known . . .

. . . there are **few financial consultants** or private resources available that can help guide you through the financial aid process.

. . . about **state and region college tuition discounts** that allow residents to attend a college in another state without paying out-of-state tuition. See NASFAA website for details (www.nasfaa.org/State_Regional_Tuition_Exchanges).

Options to Explore When Financing a College Education . . .

1) Consider **taking out an equity line of credit on your house** because the interest you pay may be deductable (up to $100,000), you have 10–15 years to pay it back, depending on the contract, and if you need to skip a payment, the mortgage company may be more than willing to work with you.

2) Consider that a line of credit on your home may be **less risky than a Parent Plus Loan** because if you miss a payment on a Plus Loan, the government can put a lien on your house. (Note: A higher interest rate on a Parent Plus Loan can only be discharged if you qualify for total permanent disability.)

3) Consider **borrowing money** for college **against a pension plan** because there is no penalty to do so.

4) When your children are young, **consider saving money for college** by putting it **into a pension plan** where there is little risk. (Penalties can be incurred for withdrawals against a newer account.)

5) Understand that the **U.Fund /529 plans may hold some financial risk** since most are attached to the stock market.

6) Understand that the **U.Fund/529** plans are **evaluated differently by financial aid**. Today, financial aid considers any money in U.Fund/529 plans as part of your assets and then calculates your financial need. In the past, the U.Fund was not a part of the initial equation to determine aid but was used to pay the balance of college costs not covered by financial aid.

7) Recognize that you have **options to finance private student loans**. Companies such as AAA, Citizens Bank and Wells Fargo may offer discounts. Shop around.

8) If you qualify, **take** the Lifetime Learning Credit, LLC, of up to $2,000 on your income tax returns every year.

9) Recognize that when you **co-sign a loan** for college, it **lowers your credit rating** because of the debt.

10) Remember, even if you file **bankruptcy**, it **does not relieve you of** your **federal loan debt**.

11) Recognize that when you **co-sign a private loan**, there is **no forgiveness**. You are responsible for the debt even after the borrower's death. You may consider an inexpensive term life insurance policy on the borrower when you co-sign a loan

in case of the student's accidental death. (**NOTE:** In the event of a cosigner's death, some lending institutions like Sallie Mae state in the promissory note that the loan may be declared in default and due, payable in full.)

12) **School interest rates are higher** than others because the students they are loaning money to usually do not have any credit.

13) Make sure **grandparents** or relatives **do not have any bank accounts** or investments **in your student's name or social security number**. Otherwise, financial aid will include these assets when evaluating your student for financial aid.

Financial advice provided by Ron Vachon, RFP, Consumer Financial Group, Holbrook, MA.

waiting

STEP #1

Recognize that anxiety and stress levels will rise during this time.

STEP #2

Discourage your students from following any social media that post admissions standings.

STEP #3

Prepare your students for all possible outcomes.

STEP #4

Encourage your students to think about multiple scenarios for the future.

STEP #5

Explore little-known facts about the college matriculation process.

The Waiting Game

After all the visits are over and all the applications submitted, you may think: "AHHH. We can relax. The work is done. Now, we just need to wait for an answer." Unfortunately, your students are still being bombarded with college chatter everywhere they go mainly because universities release admissions decisions at different times based upon whether or not an application was filed ED, EDII, EA, Rolling Admissions, or RD. From December 15 through April 1, your students and their peers will be receiving acceptance, deferral, denial or wait-list notifications. Each decision is a reminder to high school seniors that their futures are on the line. The waiting game can prove even more stressful for your children than finding the right fit in a college and filing applications.

REALITY CHECK

To compound the tension and craziness, there are numerous social media outlets where students can go to and post their admissions statuses. For many students, especially those still waiting to hear, these social media postings can be annoying at the very least and often, even harmful. As I wrote about in Chapter #6, when Patrick was waiting to hear from a school he'd applied to early action, he found a social media vehicle that posted acceptances and immediately started reviewing it several times, daily. It about drove him nuts that other students were being accepted and he had not yet heard until I had a chance to help him understand that the university was not using a systematic approach in its release of admissions decisions. In the end, he realized that this outlet's real power was that it raised the stress level of an already anxiety-ridden high school senior.

This is an appropriate time to reiterate what a good idea it is for your students to apply to not only reach and target schools, but also likely with an early action or other non-binding application. When students know they are actually going to college, the sense of relief they feel is worth the work and cost of a few more application fees. Creating that college list that equally breaks down the universities into 1/3 Reach–Far Reach, 1/3 Target, and 1/3 Likely is essential for your teens to make thoughtful, educated choices about college admissions.

As I mentioned in the first chapter, most 17-year-olds are not mature enough to manage the college search process alone. Helping them develop a plan for the whole process early on will prove critical during the waiting game when emotions can run amok. Play out possible scenarios with your children during this time. Help them understand that denial to some of the colleges they have applied to and think they want to go to is conceivable and won't be the end of the world. Even if students are fortunate to have several excellent options, making a decision might still not be easy. Remember the mantra: best fit for your student.

REALITY CHECK

December 15 brought anxiety and a host of emotions as we awaited the illusive email from a college Victoria had applied to early decision (ED – a binding agreement). As she read the email, the tears began to fall and I wrapped her up in a hug for comfort. She hadn't said a word, but I knew she had been denied acceptance to her first choice, a university that was a reach school for her. I offered my support and helped her see that she still had so many great options. Eventually her breathing slowed and she grew calmer. After about ten minutes, she looked up at me through her big teary eyes and said, "I am not sure I wanted to go there anyway." I shook my head and said to myself, "What the heck?!" Apparently, somewhere between November 15 and December 15, she had started to have reservations about this university and doubted whether or not it would be the best choice for her. As my head spun, I thought, "Ok these tears are tears of rejection, not sadness, and, boy oh boy, did we just dodge a bullet!" Even when we think we do our due diligence as parents in this college matriculation process, there will inevitably be surprises. We must remember that these college candidates are just teenagers. They are opinionated, strong-willed and vocal about so many things, but truth be told, most are not sure what they really want. In the end, they must make tough, important decisions and will, ultimately, need to live with those decisions, but understand that they may change their minds over and over again. If Victoria had been accepted to this college, she would have gone, and I am confident she would have adjusted and been fine. If not, she would have had to explore transferring to another school. In this case, the rejection may have been a blessing in disguise!

Remember that this is truly an extraordinary developmental period for your student. Here are a few points to keep in mind:

1) Recognize that your students (and you) **may take missteps** along the way.

2) **Don't try to change your students' minds** about a particular college even though the choice may seem irrational or illogical to you.

3) **Have no regrets.** Do what needs to be done to help your students. Don't look back and say we should have . . .

4) **Expect change.** Your teenagers will likely change their minds about goals and preferences multiple times during the college matriculation process no matter what you do to prepare them.

5) **Guide your students.** Listen to them. By doing so, you help them figure out what they really want.

6) **Allow** your students to make **mistakes**. It is better for them to explore and recognize any shortcomings now rather than later.

7) **Be calm and confident** about your students' choices during the process.

8) When you want to cry in sheer frustration, **laugh** instead!

9) **Breathe.** Breathe deeply. Breathe often!

Conclusion

The college search, application and matriculation process will take you on a roller coaster ride of emotions. It is exciting, frustrating, demanding, overwhelming, joyful and bittersweet for parents and their children. I hope this book has provided you with valuable information to make the ride a little easier. I am leaving you with one last list of facts about the college process that you probably won't hear from anyone else. I send you on your way with warm wishes for a rewarding journey that will lead you to **the colleges that are the best fits for your students**.

A List of Random Facts About the College Process

1) Students' **GPA and SAT/ACT scores are most often the first** and usually the most influential factor of the college application.

2) To even be considered as a candidate for the **top tier universities**, students most likely need to score in the **700+ range per subject on the SATs** and a **32+ composite score on the ACTs** unless, of course, they have some desirable talent the university is looking for such as:

    a) **Phenomenal athleticism** and prowess in a sport. (And they are being recruited by the school.)

    b) **Unique** artistic **talent**.

    c) **A legacy** at the university.

    d) Belong to a **high profile family**.

    e) Have **talents in line** with exactly what the college is looking for that particular year. (If the college needs a tuba player that year, someone who plays the tuba well but may not have scored as high on the SATs or have as high of a GPA as other applicants may get in.)

3) There are very few **acceptance surprises** to most guidance counselors.

4) **Geography** can play a role in college acceptance if a school is seeking this kind of diversity in its student body.

5) Many **high schools are feeder schools for certain colleges**. Find out if that is the case at your child's high school. Look at past matriculations to find this answer.

6) **Financial aid and grants vary dramatically at private universities.** It may cost your student less to attend a private university than a public one.

7) **Cast a wide net of public and private school college applications** in order to compare financial aid and scholarship packages.

8) **It is not** as **easy to double major** at many universities as they make it seem. Find out specifically what is involved if your student is interested in a double major. For example, if students want to study music and business, ask what degrees they will earn. Will they graduate with a double major, or a major and minor in

Music and Economics from the Liberal Arts College or can they earn two separate degrees, one in Music from the Liberal Arts College and one in Business from the Business School?

9) Many high schools, both public and private, have a computer program called **Naviance** that tracks acceptance rates of past students. This program identifies key factors such as the GPAs and SAT scores of students who have been accepted or denied admittance from your child's particular high school. It is the best way to see exactly what a student from the school needs in terms of grades and test scores in order to even be considered for a particular college.

REALITY CHECK

I discovered that Naviance takes scores and data from former students of my teens' high schools and visually plots the information on a line graph and can then add my children's scores to illustrate exactly where they fell in the spectrum. Depending on the high school's policy, students and parents might have access to this program. Ask the high school college counselor if Naviance is an available college admissions tool at your child's high school. It is important to remember that Naviance is limited because it only gives you information based upon colleges that graduates from your student's high school have attended in the past.

10) **Creating a college list of schools** to which your students will actually apply is a process that evolves. The number of colleges students apply to nationally averages 3.14 while experts in the field generally recommend students apply to 5–8 universities. If you and your teens have worked with your guidance departments, visited some college campuses, done some independent research, and utilized resources such as Naviance, the College Scorecard (collegescorecard.ed.gov), the Fiske Guide or Peterson's Review (www.petersons.com), the **college list** will begin **to narrow** over the summer before senior year. By the fall of senior year, your teens will have matured, will be more self-aware and will be more educated about the admission process.

Their final list should be broken equally down into schools that fall in three categories; **1/3 Reach–far reach, 1/3 Target, 1/3 Likely**. The next step would be to quality this list. Teens should make sure that these 7–8 colleges they have chosen to apply to are their **"Favorites"** and that they **"Like their Likelies"**! If not, teens should tweak this list further. This equally weighted list should foster a calmer teen moving through the application process because they will know that they have pushed themselves but also have planned for alternative paths. The goal here for parents is to guide your teens to a place in the admissions process that helps then recognize what **"Colleges are the Best Fit,"** academically and financially!

11) **Independent College Consultants** often have vast experience in college admissions so they may be able to provide unique insight into the college search process. Typically, they are familiar with programs and fields of study at an array of colleges across the country. Often, independent consultants can identify what credentials a student needs to gain acceptance into certain prestigious universities. Additionally, they may specialize in working with a certain group of candidates seeking college admissions (athletes, artists, scholars). A college consultant offers guidance and support for the parents and their college-bound students while taking a lot of the pressure and parent/child confrontations off the table. Some independent college consultants require students to begin working with them as early as sophomore year in high school. The cost to employ one is minimally a couple of thousand dollars.

REALITY CHECK

In the spring of Aly's junior year in high school, I heard from so many friends and acquaintances about how they had hired a college consultant for their students. I had no clue what I was doing and at that point had not made any progress with my daughter on the college front. I collected a few referrals and made some calls. Once I processed the costs for these professional services, I tried to figure out what they could really offer us. It took me a couple of months to convince my husband to even entertain the idea of hiring a consultant, but he finally acquiesced and we made an appointment with one who came highly recommended. (This consultant happened to be part of a national organization.) What we discovered in that meeting was that, yes, he could make the process easier for us because we didn't want to be policing Aly's every move and would still be informed about her progress. The college consultant could offer a list of recommended schools, help Aly with the applications and essays, and, perhaps best of all, she would be accountable to him, not us. This alone is a great service if you have the funds and don't have the time or energy to stay on top of your students as they go through the college search, but I was looking for more. I wanted Aly to have help figuring out what she really wanted and support her as she moved through an extremely emotionally charged time in her life. I knew the college consultant was not going to able to (and probably should not) provide that kind of help. It was us who were going to have to step up and be there for her—take her on those college visits, listen to her feelings and guide her in making a good decision. We were fortunate that Aly was willing to let us guide her. Not all parents and teens can agree on direction and boundaries when it comes to college admissions.

12) **Post Graduate (PG)/Gap Year.** I have already written about post graduate (PG) and gap years as they pertain to sports but feel it's fitting to mention them again here. As you no doubt know, post graduate (PG) years and gap years are often used interchangeably to reference the year or two after high school when a student takes some time off before attending college. Students choose to take PGs or Gap years after high school for several reasons. They may have been accepted to a college for the next calendar year. This happens more often at prestigious universities that have a pool of qualified candidates they want to accept but do not have enough room for in the current freshman class. During this interval, students often sign up for a year of service or try to get an internship in an area of interest. Another reason students take gap years is that they or their parents believe they are not quite ready for college for either financial reasons or because of maturity. Often, these students have been accepted to a university but are deferring enrollment until a future date. In this interval, students usually look for jobs or volunteer opportunities within their communities. Again, a tactic many students use to get into a more prestigious school than they think they can get into right after high school is to enroll in a college preparatory school where they continue to take high school classes with the hope of improving their academic standing. Athletes who want to hone their talent in a particular sport may also choose to attend college preparatory schools right after high school in order to play in a good college. Experts recommend that if your teens are considering a gap year outside of the traditional preparatory school, they should apply to college during senior year of high school, choose the college they would like to attend and then defer enrollment for one year.

REALITY CHECK

A PG year can be a useful tool if it fits in with your student's long term goals. I know a young woman who was accepted to Harvard but her enrollment was deferred for one year. She chose to accept the offer and enjoyed a meaningful and relaxed gap year.

Today, taking a PG or gap year is not uncommon. Many teens are orchestrating gap years while setting goals and working towards a career, academic, service or adventure experience where personal growth and maturity are a priority.

In this free market economy, PG years and gap years have gone commercial. There are now companies that offer exciting programs for students between high school and college. When I googled PG/Gap year options, about 572,000,000 entities popped up in .54 seconds. The possibilities for a PG or gap year are endless if you have the desire, interest and resources for your students to take one. Since a PG or a gap year is such a personal decision, any of these options should be evaluated on an individual basis. A good place to start for information about PG/gap years is Gap Year Association (www.gapyearassociation.org).

13) **Social media** can have an impact on college admissions if a student exhibits bad behavior and makes it easy for all to see. Admissions personnel, just like future employers, have the ability to check out a student on social media sites if they choose to do so. Why give admissions any ammunition to deny your student? Keep social networking safe, clean and legal!

REALITY CHECK

The implications of social media on college applications have changed drastically over the last ten years. Ten years ago, Facebook was the rage and every teenager had a page and publicly shared every picture of every event in their lives whether their conduct was innocent or illegal. I remember the story of a high school athletic team being benched for the play-offs because a parent found a picture on Facebook that showed the group involved in underage drinking. I remember thinking, "How dumb are these kids?!" Back then my motto was "Whatever you put on Facebook is there for the whole world to see." At that time, it was fairly easy for anyone, including college admissions officers, to gain access to a candidate's Facebook page. Knowing this, I admit that I scrutinized Aly's page. Two years later, when Patrick was applying to college, Facebook was still the most visible of the social media options with Twitter gaining momentum. Again, I focused most of my attention on reminding Patrick to keep his Facebook page clean in case an admissions administrator looked. With the onset of Instagram, Snapchat and Vine, I have been left behind. What I do know is that you can make your Twitter, Instagram, Snapchat and Vine accounts public or private. For the most part, it is not as easy to look at someone's tweets or pictures if the account is private. Current high school students are definitely more savvy than their parents and they can be discreet when it comes to sharing information because they have seen upperclassmen lose admission and scholarships to colleges due to internet proof of bad behavior. I now rely on something I learned at a forum on social media over ten years ago. The point that this group of professionals drove home to parents was the need to educate your children to the potential problems and consequences of sharing information on social media. With new social media options available constantly, this generation is always going to be more advanced than their parents. So what are we to do? We have to remember that teenagers are hard wired to make bad decisions. By accepting this, we can work with them to keep them happy and safe. Throughout her high school years, I talked to Victoria and tried to educate her about the implications of social media and feel that I now must rely on her own instincts to protect herself from bad choices that could have dire consequences. I know I was and will never be able to outsmart Victoria or my tenth-grader, Reece, on the social media front but I do know that if I educate them, always holding them accountable, make sure they are safe and let them know that they are loved, then the lessons they learn from that will roll over into their activity on social media. My goal is to teach them to think and make good choices in everything they do.

14) **Honors and Scholars Programs.** Most universities have honors or scholars programs for select students. Students may automatically be considered as freshmen applicants to these programs if they have a certain GPA or standardized test scores, but, in some cases, they may apply independently. Most applications require a writing supplement, typically in which students explain why they would be good candidates. Additionally, an interview may be required. Usually honors or scholars programs have more demanding course work, have GPA requirements and offer students additional benefits including research opportunities, unique courses and housing in more desirable accommodations. Some universities even allow upperclassmen to enroll in honors programs. Check with your students' universities if these programs could be an option for them.

NOTE: Some universities, such as Indiana University, identify merit scholarships for certain GPAs in the Financial Aid section of their website.

REALITY CHECK

My charming, charismatic nephew just finished his senior year in a Scholars Program at a Midwestern state college. As a high school student, he applied to the honors and scholars program using the Common Application. He was required to write a short supplement where he evaluated the goals of the program as it related to his own studies as well as the benefits of being a part of the program. Eventually, he received an email and a letter stating his admission into the Scholars Program. He was given a list of options within the program and had to submit his top choices. He choose programs based upon his intended major and is currently enrolled in a business curriculum that gives him specialization and scheduling privileges, an additional advisor and a unique housing opportunity. (He lived in a "learning community" with 58 of his fellow scholars.) Additional benefits of the Scholars Program include early move in, socializing, networking and an extra class that incorporates resume building, study tips, campus resources, etc. He had specific academic and extra-curricular requirements including a minimum GPA, citizen programs, workshops and community service. Overall, his experience was very positive. The scholars program has helped him in every aspect of his first year of college. He explained, "Not knowing anyone, it gave me a great network of awesome people to live with and get to know."

Some universities offer participation in Honors and Scholars programs in concert with grants or scholarships to attract academically superior students. As families struggle to finance college tuition and students look for the best path to a successful future, honors programs are becoming more and more attractive.

Epilogue

MARCH 2019

Aly Clark enrolled at Hobart and William Smith Colleges in Geneva, New York as a freshman in 2011. She rowed for the William Smith Crew Team throughout her four years of college. She graduated in May, 2015, with Bachelor of Arts Degree with a major in Anthropology and a minor in Health Professions. Both Aly and I agree that HWS was a good fit for her. As an athlete, her college life was demanding, but her road has been one of much growth in maturity and compassion. Aly's high school and college years have taught me to be a better listener. (**NOTE:** Aly has been living and working in NYC since graduation and is currently employed by a large international corporation in marketing.)

Patrick Clark attended Tulane University and graduated in May of 2017 with a BFA in vocal performance and a BS in Business Administration. Both Patrick and I whole-heartedly agree that Tulane was a great fit for him. It has exposed him to new cultures and many aspects of the music industry. He kept himself busy with academics, voice lessons and music, performing with Tulane's *a capella* group, Green Envy, and various theater groups. He was not sure exactly what his path would be after graduation but he constantly put himself out there and explored opportunities in the music industry. The college process with Patrick taught me to dream big (this book) and has reminded me to keep the faith. (**NOTE:** Patrick is a candidate for a masters degree in Music at NYU Steinhardt School. He will graduate in May 2019. He plans to pursue a career in musical theater.)

Victoria Clark matriculated from Buckingham, Browne and Nichols High School in Cambridge, MA, in 2015 and is currently a senior at Tulane University in New Orleans. Even though she applied to several colleges, she decided to follow her brother to Tulane University where she is studying psychology, history and French. Although their goals were different, Victoria and Patrick have similar personalities so it didn't really surprise me that she felt such a strong connection to Tulane. In my opinion, the familiarity of the campus, the variety and strong academic programs and the bond she shares with Patrick made it an easy choice for her. Going through the college process with her reminded me that each of our children is unique. They have their own ideas and needs that should be addressed and treated individually (even if they do end up in the same place as their siblings). (**NOTE:** Victoria will graduate in May 2019 with a BS in psychology, a major in history and a minor in French. She will return to Boston to pursue a career in business.)

Reece Clark is a sophomore at Northfield Mount Herman School in Mount Herman, MA. He is a bright, energetic, athletic young man who loves basketball and dreams of playing in college. As he watched his siblings wade the waters of the college process with me, Reece reminded me to live in the moment and laugh more often, especially during stressful times. His passion has also reaffirmed my renewed belief to dream big but to do so in an atmosphere that still focuses on and promotes intellect, boundaries, consequences and respect.

appendix a

TOP FIVE TIPS FOR COLLEGE ADMISSIONS

- ☐ **Set up separate email accounts** for parent and student for all college communications.
- ☐ **Set up a weekly meeting** with your teen, starting junior year.
- ☐ Create a **schedule and a timeline** with your teen.
- ☐ **Record all college** visits in a notebook or visit sheet.
- ☐ **Guide your teen** toward colleges that are the best fit academically and financially!

appendix b

Junior Year Checklists

September

- [ ] Set up a **separate email account** for all college correspondence.
- [ ] Take the **PSAT** in the fall. (Typically offered by student's high school.)
- [ ] Set up a mutually agreeable **weekly meeting** with your teen.

October–November

- [ ] **Research colleges** based upon interests and academics.
  - [ ] U.S. Dept. of Education: www.collegescorecard.ed.gov.
  - [ ] Guidebooks: Petersons (www.petersons.com), Fiske (www.fiske. sourcebookscollege.com), Princeton Review (www.princetonreview.com/ college-education).
  - [ ] Naviance—offered through individual high schools.
- [ ] Create a **College Board Account** to register for the SAT (www.collegeboard.com).
- [ ] Create an **ACT account** to register and review for ACT (www.actstudent.com).

December

- [ ] Develop a tentative **schedule** for taking **standardized tests**. (SAT/ACT/Subject Tests).
- [ ] Set up **time** or **tutoring** to prepare for standardized tests.

January

- ☐ Continue to **research colleges** based upon interests and academics.
- ☐ Develop a tentative **schedule** for **college visits** over breaks or weekends.
- ☐ **Develop a list** of colleges to visit based upon research.
- ☐ **Sign up** for Spring **SAT/ACT/Subject Tests**.

February–March

- ☐ **Visit colleges**, local or long distance, over school breaks.
- ☐ Continue to **research colleges** based upon interests and academics.

April–May

- ☐ Ask at least **two teachers** for a college **recommendation**.
- ☐ Continue **to research colleges** based upon interests and academics.
- ☐ Access your **list of colleges** that will be a **"good fit"** academically and financially.
- ☐ Develop a **schedule** for **college visits** over the summer based upon that list.

June

- ☐ Determine if you will take the **SAT/ACT/Subject Tests** in the **summer** or the fall.
- ☐ **Sign up** for August SAT/ACT/Subject Tests.
- ☐ Develop a **schedule** for taking, tutoring or **preparing** for standardized tests.

appendix c

Senior Year Checklists

Summer Rising Seniors

June–July
- [ ] Reassess **list of colleges** that will be a **"good fit"** academically and financially.
- [ ] Fine-tune the **schedule** for **college visits** over the summer.
- [ ] Continue to **research colleges** based upon interests and academics.

August
- [ ] Develop a **rough draft** for the Common Application **essay**.
- [ ] **Fill out** student and family information on the **Common App**.
- [ ] Continue to **narrow** choices of **colleges list**.

September
- [ ] **Confirm** teacher **recommendations**.
- [ ] Ask a teacher or guidance counselor to **review** your Common App essay.
- [ ] Sign up for **SAT/ACT tests** or subjects tests scheduled for the **fall**.
- [ ] Continue to **narrow** choices of the **college list**.
- [ ] **Schedule** local **college visits** for Saturday in the fall or over holiday day weekend.
- [ ] Schedule **interviews** with universities or alumni where applicable.
- [ ] **Develop final** college list.

October

- ☐ Access **additional essay requirements** by colleges.
- ☐ Begin to **work on additional, college specific, essays**.
- ☐ Begin to evaluate **timing of applications**. (Early Decision, Early Action or Regular Decision).
- ☐ **Decide on timing** of applications.

November

- ☐ Submit **early decision** or early **action applications**.
- ☐ Continue to **work** on additional college **essays** and all other **applications**.
- ☐ **Access college list.**

December

- ☐ Continue **to work** on additional college **essays** and all other **applications**.
- ☐ **Finalize college list.**
- ☐ **Submit regular decision** applications.

appendix d

College Visit Checklists

Before A College Visit

- [ ] **Research majors** offered at each university.
- [ ] **Sign up for student run blogs or newspapers.**
- [ ] Find out if there are **special tours** offered for different majors (e.g. arts or engineering).
- [ ] Find out if **Financial Aid** information sessions are offered.
- [ ] **Set up appointments** for tours and Information sessions with Admissions department.
- [ ] **Sign up** for student **interviews** if offered or encouraged.
- [ ] If you are an aspiring athlete, **contact the coach** and set up a meeting.
- [ ] Find out if a **parking pass** is required when visiting campus.
- [ ] **Print** a campus **map**.

Once On Campus

- [ ] Drive and/or **walk around** the campus and surrounding neighborhoods.
- [ ] **Eat** at a **local** restaurant or in the college cafeteria.
- [ ] **Ask** all university representatives **questions** about issues or concerns.

Insider Tips

- [ ] See if you can **meet a current student** from your town or high school for coffee or lunch.
- [ ] Pick up a **school newspaper.**
- [ ] Sign up for **student run blogs** or electronic news platforms.
- [ ] **Explore** whether the College offers **internship programs** for students.
- [ ] Stop by career development office to explore **networking opportunities** and post graduation **employment.**
- [ ] Find out the name of the **Regional Coordinator** that is assigned to your high school.
- [ ] Before you leave, **record all impressions** of the College visited.

appendix e

Financial Aid Suggested Timeline Senior Year

August

- ☐ **Activate an FSA ID.** (used to file FAFSA)
- ☐ **Review FAFSA** available by August 1.
- ☐ **Review CSS/PROFILE.**
- ☐ Attend a **college financial aid session** while visiting schools with your students.
- ☐ **Look** for any **resources** offering financial aid seminars. (Local high school, community organizations, webinars from universities or nonprofits)
- ☐ **Gather pertinent documents** needed to fill out the FAFSA and CSS/Profile.
- ☐ Includes: social security number, driver's license number, W-2 forms and other records of taxed and untaxed income, bank statements on savings and investments from 2 years prior.

September

- ☐ **Print** a copy of the FAFSA
- ☐ **Set aside** plenty of **time** to fill out the FAFSA.
- ☐ Give yourself a **deadline** for completing the **FAFSA** based upon the college requirements.
- ☐ **Gather** additional **documents** needed to fill out the CSS/PROFILE.
- ☐ **Set aside** plenty of **time** to fill out the **CSS/PROFILE**. It can be filled out online and saved for further edits and completion.
- ☐ Give yourself a **deadline** for completing the **CSS/PROFILE** based upon the college deadlines.

October

- [ ] **Submit** the **FAFSA** on or after October 1 at www.FAFSA.ed.gov. (Important for financial aid or merit offers for early acceptance programs.)
- [ ] **Print** a copy of your FAFSA and file it for your records.
- [ ] Receive your **Expected Family Contribution (EFC)** that is calculated from the data reported on your FAFSA.
- [ ] Receive your **Student Aid Report (SAR)** from FAFSA.
- [ ] **Submit** the **CSS/Profile** on or after **October 1** at www.student.collegeboard.org/css-financial-aid-profile. (Important for financial aid or merit offers for early acceptance programs.)
- [ ] **Print** a copy of your CSS/PROFILE and file it for your records.
- [ ] Receive a **Data Confirmation Report** from CSS/PROFILE.

November

- [ ] Continue to **review financial aid options** by viewing webinars offered by colleges or third party companies.
- [ ] **Attend** any college **financial aid seminars** that you have learned about through your high school, your community or the universities your teen is interested in attending.
- [ ] **Explore merit** and affiliated **scholarships** at universities, community organizations and places of employment.

December

- [ ] Look for preliminary **Financial Aid awards** to become available for students who applied early acceptance to college and whose parents filed the FAFSA, the CSS/PROFILE or the individual university's financial aid forms.
- [ ] **File FAFSA** and **CSS/Profile** by **December 31** for most lucrative financial aid awards. (Remember: Financial aid *is* limited.)

January–April

- [ ] Students should expect to **receive Financial Aid Awards** from each college they applied to.
- [ ] **Financial Aid** award **letters** will be distributed **with or after students** are **accepted** to a university.
- [ ] Financial **Aid** award letters will be **released at different times** based upon when the application was submitted—ED, EA or RD.

May 1

☐ Students need to **accept, deny or appeal** the financial aid offers they have been given.

June–August

☐ **College** tuition **bills** received.

☐ Set up a **payment plan** with a university.

notes

Chapter #4: Applying to College

1. The Common Application. The Common Application, 2018. Web. 17 Nov. 2018. <https://www.commonapp.org/about-us>.
2. The Coalition for College. The Coalition for College, 2018. Web. 28 Nov. 2018. <https://www.commonapp.org/about-us>.
3. SlideRoom + The Common Application. SlideRoom + The Common Application, 2018. Web. 14 Nov. 2018. <http://www.slideroom.com/commonapp/guide.html>.
4. The Universal Application. Application Online, LLC, 2018. Web. 14 Nov. 2018. <https://www.universalcollegeapp.com/resources#forms>.
5. The Universal Application. Application Online, LLC, 2018. Web. 14 Nov. 2018. <https://www.universalcollegeapp.com/documents/uca-arts-supplement.pdf>.
6. SlideRoom + The Common Application. SlideRoom + The Common Application, 2018. Web. 14 Nov. 2018. <https://appsupport.commonapp.org/applicantsupport/s/article/portfolio-requirement-wsankvli>.
7. The Universal Application. Application Online, LLC, 2018. Web. 14 Nov. 2018. <https://www.universalcollegeapp.com/resources#forms>.
8. The Coalition for College. The Coalition for College, 2018. Web. 28 Nov. 2018. <http://coalitionforcollegeaccess.org/faq.html>.

Chapter #5: Standardized Testing

1. Lewin, Tamar. "Testing, Testing More Students Taking Both the ACT and SAT." nytimes.com. The New York Times, 2 Aug. 2013. Web. 17 Nov. 2018. <http://www.nytimes.com/2013/08/04/education/edlife/more-students-are-taking-both-the- act-and-sat.html?_r=0>.a
2. The Princeton Review. The Princeton Review, 2018. Web. 13 Nov. 2018. <http://usatoday30.usatoday.com/news/ education/2007-03-18-life-cover-acts_N.htm>.

3. CollegeBoard/SAT. The SAT Student Guide 2018-19, 2018. Web. 18 Nov. 2018.
    <https://collegereadiness.collegeboard.org/pdf/sat-student-guide.pdf>.

4. CollegeBoard/SAT. The SAT Student Guide 2018-19, 2018. Web. 18 Nov. 2018.
    <https://collegereadiness.collegeboard.org/pdf/sat-student-guide.pdf>.

5. CollegeBoard/SAT. The SAT Student Guide 2018-19, 2018. Web. 18 Nov. 2018.
    <https://collegereadiness.collegeboard.org/pdf/sat-student-guide.pdf>.

6. ACT. ACT Inc., 2018. Web. 20 Nov. 2018. <http://www.act.org/content/act/en/
    products-and-services.html>.

7. ACT. ACT Inc., 2018 Web 20, 2018. <http://www.act.org/content/act/en/
    products-and-services/the-act.html l>.

8. PrepScholar. PrepScholar. 2013–2018. Web. 25 Nov. 2018. <https://blog.
    prepscholar.com/good-act-score-for-2018>.

Chapter #6: Submitting the Application

1. The Common Application Applicant Solution Center. The Common
    Application, 2018. Web. 16 Dec. 2018. <https://appsupport.commonapp.org/
    applicantsupport/s/article/When-is-the-deadline-for-my-application-submission>.

Chapter #7: Athletics

1. Scholarship Stats.com. 'Average Athletic Scholarships per College Athlete', "n.d."
    Web. 22 Dec. 2018. <www.scholarshipstats.com/average-per-athlete.html.>.

2. NCAA. National Collegiate Athletic Association, "n.d." Web. 26 Dec. 2018.
    <http://www.ncaa.org/about/who-we-are/office-president/office-president-mark>.

3. NCAA. National Collegiate Athletic Association, "n.d." Web. 26
    Dec. 2018. <http://www.ncaa.org/about/resources/research/
    probability-competing-beyond-high-school>.

4. NCAA. National Collegiate Athletic Association, "n.d." Web. 26 Dec. 2018.
    <http://www.ncaa.org/about/resources/media-center/ncaa-101/what-ncaa>.

5. NCAA. National Collegiate Athletic Association, "n.d." Web. 26 Dec. 2019.
    <http://www.ncaa.org/about?division=d2>.

6. NCAA. National Collegiate Athletic Association, "n.d." Web. 5 May 2015.
    <http:// www.ncaa.org/d3>.

7. NAIA. National Association of Intercollegiate Athletics,
    "n.d." Web. 26 Dec. 2018. <http://www.naia.org/ViewArticle.
    dbml?DB_OEM_ID=27900&ATCLID=205323019>.

8. NJCAA. National Junior College Athletic Association, 2018. Web. 26 Dec. 2018.
    <http://njcaa.org/about/mission/Mission_statement>.

Chapter #8: Overview of the Financial Aid Process

1. Hess, Abigail. "Here's how much the average student loan borrower owes when they graduate." CNBC.com. CNBC Make It, 15 Feb. 2018. Web. 14 Jan. 2019. <https://www.cnbc.com/2018/02/15/heres-how-much-the-average-student-loan-borrower-owes-when-they-graduate.html>.

2. Akers, Beth. and Matthew M. Chingos. "Is Student Loan Crisis on the Horizon?" Brown Center on Education Policy at Brookings, Jun. 2014. Web. 14 Jan. 2019. <http://www.brookings.edu/~/media/research/files/reports/2014/06/24%20 student%20loan%20crisis%20akers%20chingos/is%20a%20student%20loan%20 crisis%20on%20the%20horizon.pdf>.

3. Akers, Beth. and Matthew M. Chingos. "Is Student Loan Crisis on the Horizon?" Brown Center on Education Policy at Brookings, Jun. 2014. Web. 14 Jan. 2019. <http://www.brookings.edu/~/media/research/files/reports/2014/06/24%20 student%20loan%20crisis%20akers%20chingos/is%20a%20student%20loan%20 crisis%20on%20the%20horizon.pdf>.

4. Federal Student Aid. U.S Department of Education, "n.d." Web. 14 Jan. 2019. <https://studentaid.ed.gov/sa/eligibility/infographic-accessible>.

5. Federal Student Aid. U.S Department of Education, "n.d." Web.14 Jan. 2019. <https://studentaid.ed.gov/sa/eligibility/infographic-accessible>.

6. "Massachusetts No Interest Loan Program." Massachusetts Department of Higher Education, Office of Student Financial Assistance, 2000-2019. Web. 14 Jan. 2019. <http://www.mass.edu/osfa/programs/nointerest.asp>.

7. Federal Student Aid. U.S Department of Education, "n.d." Web. 14 Jan. 2019. <https://fafsa.ed.gov/help/costatt.htm>.

8. Federal Student Aid. U.S Department of Education. "n.d." Web. 14 Jan. 2019. <https://studentaid.ed.gov/sa/fafsa/estimate>.

9. Federal Student Aid. U.S Department of Education, "n.d." Web. 14 Jan. 2019. <https://studentaid.ed.gov/glossary#Federal_Student_Aid_Programs>.

10. Onink, Troy. 2017-2018 Guide To College Financial Aid, The FAFSA And CSS Profile. Forbes 8 Jan. 2017. Web 14 Jan. 2019. <https://www.forbes.com/sites/troyonink/2017/01/08/2017-guide-to-college-financial-aid-the-fafsa-and-css-profile/#136c41204cd4>.

Chapter #9: Federal Financial Aid

1. Federal Student Aid. U.S Department of Education, "n.d." Web. 20 Jan. 2019. <https://studentaid.ed.gov/types/grants-scholarships/pell>.

2. Federal Student Aid. U.S Department of Education, "n.d." Web. 20 Jan. 2019. <https://studentaid.ed.gov/types/grants-scholarships/pell>.

3. Federal Student Aid. U.S Department of Education, "n.d." Web. 20 Jan. 2019. <https://studentaid.ed.gov/types/grants-scholarships/pell>.

4. Federal Student Aid. U.S Department of Education, "n.d." Web. 20 Jan. 2019. <https://studentaid.ed.gov/types/grants-scholarships/fseog>.

5. Federal Student Aid. U.S Department of Education, "n.d." Web. 20 Jan. 2019. <https://studentaid.ed.gov/types/grants-scholarships/teach>.
6. Federal Student Aid. U.S Department of Education, "n.d." Web. 20 Jan. 2019. <https://studentaid.ed.gov/types/grants-scholarships/teach>.
7. Federal Student Aid. U.S Department of Education, "n.d." Web. 20 Jan. 2019. <https://studentaid.ed.gov/types/grants-scholarships/teach>.
8. Federal Student Aid. U.S Department of Education, "n.d." Web. 20 Jan. 2019. <https://studentaid.ed.gov/types/grants-scholarships/teach>.
9. Federal Student Aid. U.S Department of Education, "n.d." Web. 20 Jan. 2019. <https://studentaid.ed.gov/types/grants-scholarships/teach>.
10. Federal Student Aid. U.S Department of Education, "n.d." Web. 20 Jan. 2019. <https://studentaid.ed.gov/types/grants-scholarships/teach>.
11. Federal Student Aid. U.S Department of Education, "n.d." Web. 20 Jan. 2019. <https://studentaid.ed.gov/sa/types/grants-scholarships/iraq-afghanistan-service#eligibility>.
12. Federal Student Aid. U.S Department of Education, "n.d." Web. 20 Jan. 2019. <https://studentaid.ed.gov/sa/types/grants-scholarships/iraq-afghanistan-service#eligibility>.
13. Federal Student Aid. U.S Department of Education, "n.d." Web.20 Jan. 2019. <https://studentaid.ed.gov/sa/types/grants-scholarships/iraq-afghanistan-service#eligibility>.
14. Federal Student Aid. U.S. Department of Education, Web. 21 Jan. 2019. <https://studentaid.ed.gov/sa/types/loans/plus#how-much>.
15. FinAid: The SmartStudent Guide to Financial Aid. 2019. Web. 21 Jan. 2019. <http://www.finaid.org/loans/studentloandiscounts.phtml>.
16. Federal Student Aid. U.S. Department of Education, "n.d." Web. 21 Jan. 2019. <https://studentaid.ed.gov/sa/repay-loans/consolidation#interest-rate>>.
17. Federal Student Aid. U.S Department of Education, "n.d." Web. 21 Jan. 2019. <https://studentaid.ed.gov/sa/repay-loans/consolidation>.
18. Federal Student Aid. U.S Department of Education, "n.d." Web. 21 Jan. 2019. <https://studentaid.ed.gov/sa/types/loans/perkins>.

Chapter #10: State College, and Private Financial Aid

1. National Association of Student Financial Aid Administrators. "N.p." "n.d." Web. 21 Jan. 2019. <https://www.nasfaa.org/About_NASFAA>.
2. National Association of Student Financial Aid Administrators. "N.p." "n.d." Web. 21 Jan. 2019. <https://www.nasfaa.org/About_NASFAA>.
3. "Student Financial Services." Carnegie Mellon University: Division of Enrollment Services. Carnegie Mellon University, 2019. Web. 21 Jan. 2019. <https://www.cmu.edu/sfs/financial-aid/undergraduate/>.

4. "Scholarships & Financial Aid." Washington University in St. Louis Undergraduate Admissions. Washington University in St. Louis, 2019. Web. 21 Jan. 2019. <https://admissions.wustl.edu/Financial_Aid_Scholarships/Need_Based_Financial_Aid/Pages/First-Year-Students.aspx>.

5. "Types of Financial Aid." Stanford: Financial Aid. Stanford University, "n.d." Web. 21 Jan. 2019. <https://financialaid.stanford.edu/undergrad/types/index.html>.

6. O'Shaughnessy, Lynn. "Do college scholarships search engines work?" CBS Money Watch, 8 Oct. 2013. Web. 24 Nov. 2019. <http://www.cbsnews.com/news/ do-college-scholarship-search-engines-work/>.

7. Looney, Adam. "More Students are taking on crippling debt they can't repay-it's time for higher education to share the risks." Brookings, Feb. 2018: 3. Web. 22 Jan. 2019. <https://www.brookings.edu/blog/up-front/2018/02/16/more-students-are-taking-on-crippling-debt-they-cant-repay-its-time-for-higher-education-to-share-the-risks/>.

8. Friedman, Zack. "Student Loan Debt Statistics in 2018: A $1.5 Trillion Crisis." Forbes, Jun. 2018. Web. 23 Jan. 2019. <https://www.forbes.com/sites/zackfriedman/2018/06/13/student-loan-debt-statistics-2018/#5ef4b2b97310>.

works cited

Act.org. ACT Inc., 2018. Web. 15 Dec. 2018. <http://www.act.org/content/act/en/ products-and-services/the-act/scores/understanding-your-scores.html>.

Act.org. ACT Inc., 2018. Web. 15 Dec. 2018. <http://www.act.org/content/dam/act/ unsecured/documents/UsingYourACTResults2018-19.pdf>.

Act.org. ACT Inc., 2018. Web. 15 Dec. 2018. Act Test Scores <https://blog. prepscholar.com/good-act-score-for-2018.>

Admissions.cornell.edu. Cornell University: Undergraduate Admissions. Cornell University, 2018. Web. 19 Dec. 2018. <https://admissions.cornell.edu/ standardized-testing-requirements>.

Admissions.indiana.edu. Indiana University Bloomington: Office of Admissions. The Trustees of Indiana University, 2019. Web. 2. Feb. 2019. <https://admissions. indiana.edu/apply/freshman/index.html>.

Admission.stanford.edu. Stanford University: Undergraduate Admission. Stanford University, 2018. Web. 19 Dec. 2018. <https://admission.stanford.edu/apply/ decision_process/index.html>.

Admissions.umd.edu. University of Maryland: Office of Undergraduate Admissions. University of Maryland, 2018. Web. 19 Dec. 2018. <https://admissions.umd.edu/ apply/application-deadlines>.

Admission.universityofcalifornia.edu. University of California: Admissions. Regents of the University of California, 2018. Web. 19 Dec. 2018. <http://admission. universityofcalifornia.edu/how-to-apply/apply-online/>.

Admissions.utah.edu. The University of Utah: Office of Admissions. The University of Utah, 2019. Web. 4 Feb. 2019. <http://admissions.utah.edu/apply/ deferment/>.

Admissions.wustl.edu. Washington University in St. Louis Undergraduate Admissions: Freshman Student Financial Aid. Washington University in St. Louis, 2019. Web. 4 Feb. 2019. <https://admissions.wustl.edu/ financial-aid#overview>.

Akers, Beth. and Matthew M. Chingos. "Is Student Loan Crisis on the Horizon?" brookings.edu. Brown Center on Education Policy at Brookings, Jun. 2014. Web. 14 Jan. 2019. <http://www.brookings.edu/~/media/research/files/reports/2014/06/24%20 student%20loan%20crisis%20akers%20chingos/is%20 a%20student%20loan%20 crisis%20on%20the%20horizon.pdf>.

American.edu. American University: Financial Aid. American University, 2019. Web. 4 Feb. 2019. <http://www.american.edu/financialaid/freshmanprospects.cfm>.

Anderson, Ellen. "What is the Coalition Application?" collegeraptor.com. College Raptor, Nov. 2018. Web. 7 Dec. 2018. <https://www.collegeraptor.com/getting-in/articles/questions-answers/what-is-the-coalition-application/>.

Anderson, Nick. "As SAT enters a new era this week, students say the exam has improved. " washingtonpost.com. The Washington Post, 3 March 2016. Web. 4 Feb. 2019. <https:// www.washingtonpost.com/news/grade-point/wp/2016/03/03/as-sat-enters-a- new-era-this-week-students-say-the-exam-has-improved/?tid=a_inl>.

————. "Why your new SAT score is not as strong as you think it is." washingtonpost.com. Washington Post. 11 May 2016. Web. 5 Feb. 2019. <https:// www.washingtonpost.com/news/grade-point/wp/2016/05/11/why-your-new-sat-score-is-not-as-strong-as-you-think-it-is/?utm_term=.e004ccc46665.>.

Apstudent.collegeboard.org. The College Board, 2019. Web. 4 Feb. 2019. <https:// apstudent.collegeboard.org>.

Bc.edu. Boston College: Office of Undergraduate Admissions. The Trustees of Boston College, 2019. Web. 8 Feb. 2019. <https://www.bc.edu/content/bc-web/admission/apply.html>.

Bigfuture.collegeboard.org. Big future. The College Board, "n.d." Web. 3 Feb. 2019. <https://bigfuture.collegeboard.org/scholarship-search>.

Blog.collegegreenlight.com. College Greenlight, 2019. Web. 14 Jan. 2019. <http://blog.collegegreenlight.com/blog/colleges-that-meet-100-of-student-financial-need/#C17>.

Bowdoin.edu. Bowdoin: The Academic Handbook; Admission. Financial Aid. Bowdoin College, "n.d." Web. 3 Feb. 2019. <https://www.bowdoin.edu/academic-handbook/admission-to-the-college/financial-aid.html>.

Buckingham, Browne & Nichols School: COLLEGE COUNSELING WORKBOOK CLASS OF 2015. "n.p." "n.d." Print.

Cappex.com. Cappex, 2019 Web. 3 Feb. 2019. <https://www.cappex.com/scholarshipshttps://>.

Clubbaseball.org. National Club Baseball Association, 2016. Web. 27 Dec. 2018. <https://www.clubbaseball.org>.

Coalitionforcollegeaccess.org. The Coalition for College, 2018. Web. 9 Dec. 2018. <http://www.coalitionforcollegeaccess.org/>.

Coalitionforcollegeaccess.org. The Coalition for College, 2018. Web. 10 Dec. 2018. <http://www.coalitionforcollegeaccess.org/essays.html>.

Coalitionforcollegeaccess.org. The Coalition for College, 2018. Web. 13 Dec. 2018. <http://www.coalitionforcollegeaccess.org/alert.html>.

Coalitionforcollegeaccess.org. The Coalition for College, 2018. Web. 19 Dec. 2018. <https://coalitionlocker.zendesk.com/hc/en-us/ articles/218959707-Family-Information-Section>.

Coalitionforcollegeaccess.org. The Coalition for College, 2018. Web. 19 Dec. 2018. <https://coalitionlocker.zendesk.com/hc/en-us/ articles/218441207-Personal-Information-Section>.

Coalitionforcollegeaccess.org. The Coalition for College, 2018. Web. 19 Dec. 2018. <https://coalitionlocker.zendesk.com/hc/en-us/ articles/227068047-Quick-Start-Guide>.

Coalitionforcollegeaccess.org. The Coalition for College, 2018. Web. 27 Dec. 2018. *<http://coalitionforcollegeaccess.org/faq.html>*.

Collclubsports.com. National Club Basketball Association, 2015. Web. 27 Dec. 2018. <https://www.collclubsports.com>.

Collegeboard.org. College Board, Jan. 2019. Web. 21 Dec. 2018. <https://profile. collegeboard.org/profile/ppi/participatingInstitutions.aspx>.

Collegeboard.org. The College Board. The College Board and the National Merit Scholarship Corporation, 2018. Web. 21 Dec. 2018. <https://collegereadiness. collegeboard.org/sat-subject-tests/about/institutions-using>.

Collegeboard.org. The College Board: SAT. The College Board and the National Merit Scholarship Corporation, 2018. Web. 21 Dec. 2018. <https://secure-media. collegeboard.org/sat/pdf/sat-subject-tests-percentile-ranks.pdf>.

Collegeboard.org. The College Board: AP. The College Board and the National Merit Scholarship Corporation, 2018. Web. 14 Jan. 2019. <https://apstudent. collegeboard.org/apcourse>.

Collegescholarships.org. CollegeScholarships.org, 1999–2018. Web. 19 Feb. 2019. <http://www.collegescholarships.org/loans/state.htm>.

Collegeweeklive.com. College Week Live, 2019. Web. 4 Feb. 2019. <https://www. collegeweeklive.com>.

Commonapp.org. The Common Application, 27 Jan. 2018. Web. 9 Dec. 2018. *<https://www.commonapp.org/whats-appening/ application-updates/2018-2019-common-application-essay-prompts>*.

Commonapp.org. The Common Application, 2018. Web. 16 Dec. 2018. <https://appsupport.commonapp.org/applicantsupport/s/article/ When-is-the-deadline-for-my-application-submission>.

Commonapp.org. The Common Application, 2018. Web. 16 Dec. 2018. <https://appsupport.commonapp.org/applicantsupport/s/article/ portfolio-requirement-wsankvli>.

"Convert-a-Percentage-into-a-4.0-Grade-Point-Average." wikiHow. com. wikiHow, "n.d." Web. 5 Jan. 2019. <http://m.wikihow.com/ Convert-a-Percentage-into-a-4.0-Grade-Point-Average>.

Cmu.edu. Student Financial Services, Carnegie Mellon University: Division of Enrollment Services. Carnegie Mellon University, 2019. Web. 21 Jan. 2019. <https://www.cmu.edu/sfs/financial-aid/undergraduate/>.

Css.collegeboard.org. CSS/Financial Aid Profile, The College Board, 2019. Web. 5 Feb. 2019. <http://css.collegeboard.org/>.

Dartmouth.edu. Dartmouth College. Trustees of Dartmouth College, 2019. Web. 5 Feb. 2019. <http://www.dartmouthsports.com>.

Discoveractaspire.org. ACT, Inc., "n.d.". Web. 4 Feb. 2019. <https://www.discoveractaspire.org>.

Dix, Willard. "Digging For Scholarships can Turn Up College Gold." forbes.com. Forbes, Nov. 2016. Web. 21 Jan. 2019. <https://www.forbes.com/sites/willarddix/2016/11/01/digging-for-scholarships-can-turn-up-college-gold/#7a4e615c3cc8>.

Doster, Adam. "The Greatest Game you Have Ever Seen." Boston Magazine, Mar. 2014: 92-95. Print.

Fafsa.ed.gov. FAFSA: Free Application for Student Aid. U.S. Department of Education, "n.d." Web. 4 Feb. 2019. <https://studentaid.ed.gov/sa/fafsa>.

Fairtest.org. FairTest: The National Center for Fair and Open Testing, 2015. Web. 5 Feb. 2019. <http://www.fairtest.org/university/optional)>.

Fastweb.com. fastweb!. Fastweb. "n.d." Web. 15 Nov. 2018. <https://www.fastweb.com/>.

Federalreserve.gov. The Governors of the FEDERAL RESERVE SYSTEM, 14 Jun. 2017. Web. 14 Jan. 2019. <https://www.federalreserve.gov/publications/2017-economic-well-being-of-us-households-in-2016-education-debt-loans.htm>.

Finaid.org. "Loan Calculator." FinAid: The Smart Student's Guide to Financial Aid. finaid.org. FinAid Page, LLC, 2019. Web. 2 Feb. 2019. <http://www.finaid.org/calculators/scripts/loanpayments.cgi>.

Friedman, Zack. "Student Loan Debt Statistics in 2018: A $1.5 Trillian Crisis. " forbes.com. Forbes, Jun. 2018. Web. 23 Jan. 2019. <https://www.forbes.com/sites/zackfriedman/2018/06/13/student-loan-debt-statistics-2018/#5ef4b2b97310>.

fsaid.ed.gov. Federal Student Aid. U.S. Department of Education, "n.d." Web. 5 Feb. 2019. <https://fsaid.ed.gov/npas/index.htm>.

Irs.gov. Education Credits-AOTC and LLC. IRS, "n.d." Web. 24 Jan. 2019. <https://www.irs.gov/credits-deductions/individuals/llc>.

Lewin, Tamar. "Testing, Testing More Students Taking Both the ACT and SAT." nytimes.com. The New York Times, 2 Aug. 2013. Web. 17 Nov. 2018. <http://www.nytimes.com/2013/08/04/education/edlife/more-students-are-taking-both-the- act-and-sat.html?_r=0>.

Looney, Adam. "More Students are taking on crippling debt they can't repay-it's time for higher education to share the risks." brookings.edu. Brookings, Feb. 2018: 3. Web. 22 Jan. 2019. <https://www.brookings.edu/blog/up-front/2018/02/16/more-students-are-taking-on-crippling- debt-they-cant-repay-its-time-for-higher-education-to-share-the-risks/>.

Mass.edu. "Massachusetts No Interest Loan Program." Massachusetts Department of Higher Education, Office of Student Financial Assistance, "n.d." Web. 5 Feb. 2019. <http://www.mass.edu/osfa/programs/nointerest.asp>.

Muniz, Hannah. "What's a Good ACT Score for 2018?" prepscholar.com.
PrepScholar, Nov. 2017. Web. 8 Dec. 2018. <https://blog.prepscholar.com/
good-act-score-for-2018>.

Naia.org. National Association Intercollegiate Athletics, 2018.
Web. 26 Dec. 2018. <http://www.naia.org/ViewArticle.
dbml?DB_OEM_ID=27900&ATCLID=211220537>.

Naia.org. National Association Intercollegiate Athletics, 2018. Web. 26
Dec. 2018. <http://www.naia.org/ViewArticle.dbml?DB_LANG=C&DB_OEM_ID=2790
0&ATCLID=208532562&SPID=124108&SPSID=730210>.

Naia.org. National Association Intercollegiate Athletics, 2018. Web. 26 Dec. 2018.
<https://www.playnaia.org/eligibility-center>.

Nasfaa.org. National Association of Student Financial Aid Administrators, "n.d."
Web. 21 Jan. 2019. <https://www.nasfaa.org/About_NASFAA>.

Nationalletter.org. National Letter of Intent, 2018. Web. 26 Dec. 2018. <http://www.
nationalletter.org>.

Ncaa.org. National Collegiate Athletic Association, 2018. Web. 26 Dec. 2018.
<https://www.ncaa.org/sites/default/files/Recruiting%20Fact%20Sheet%20WEB.
pdf>.

Ncaa.org. National Collegiate Athletic Association, 2018. Web. 27 Dec. 2018. <http://
www.ncaa.org/about?division=d3>.

Ncaa.org. National Collegiate Athletic Association, 2018. Web. 27 Dec. 2018.
<https://web3.ncaa.org/ecwr3/>.

Ncaa.org. National Collegiate Athletic Association, 2018. Web. 27 Dec. 2018.
<https://web3.ncaa.org/directory/>.

Njcaa.org. National Junior College Athletic Association, 2018. Web. 26 Dec.
2018. <https://mvp.njcaa.org/DocumentsAndFiles/NjcaaForms/180723_10_
Eligibility%20Pamphlet%202018.pdf.>

Njcaa.org. National Junior College Athletic Association, 2018. Web. 26 Dec. 2018.
<http://njcaa.org/member_colleges/Divisional_Structure.>

Njcaa.org. National Junior College Athletic Association, 2018. Web. 26 Dec. 2018.
<https://d2o2figo6ddd0g.cloudfront.net/1/f/foxubphijs5cjm/NJCAA_SA_
Participation_Stats_8.1.17.pdf>.

Njcaa.org. NJCAA. National Junior College Athletic Association, "n.d." Web. 4 Feb.
2019. <http://www.njcaa.org>.

Nykiel, Teddy. "CSS Profile: Everything You Need to Know in 2019-2220." nerdwallet.
com. Nerdwallet, Dec. 2018. Web. 21 Jan. 2019. <https://www.nerdwallet.com/
blog/loans/student-loans/css-profile/>.

Onink, Troy. "2017 Guide to College Financial Aid, the FAFSA, and CSS Profile."
forbes.com. Forbes, 30 Jan. 2016. Web. 14 Jan. 2019. <https://www.forbes.com/
sites/troyonink/2017/01/08/2017-guide-to-college-financial-aid-the-fafsa-and-css-
profile/#6141c08f4cd4>.

O'Shaughnessy, Lynn. "Do college scholarships search engines work?" cbsnew.com.
CBS Money Watch, 8 Oct. 2013. Web. 24 Nov. 2019. <http://www.cbsnews.com/
news/ do-college-scholarship-search-engines-work/>.

Petersons.com. Peterson's, 2019. Web. 3 Feb. 2019. <https://www.petersons.com>.

Playnaia.org. NAIA. The NAIA Eligibility Center. National Association of Intercollegiate Athletics, "n.d." Web. 2. Jan. 2017. <www.playnaia.org>.

Princetonreview.com. The Princeton Review. "n.d.". Web. 8 Feb. 2019. <https://www.princetonreview.com/college/sat-act#>.

Recreation.richmond.edu. University of Richmond: Recreation & Wellness. University of Richmond, "n.d." Web. 4 Feb. 2019. <https://recreation.richmond.edu/clubs/active/womens-soccer.html>.

Ross, Kelly Mae. "A Complete Guide to the College Application Process." usnews,com, U.S. News, Mar. 2018. Web. 9 Dec. 2018. <https://www.usnews.com/education/best-colleges/articles/college-application-process>.

Ruppel Shell, Ellen, "Opinion - College May Not Be Worth It Anymore." nytimes.com. New York Times, 16 may, 2018. Web. 6 Feb. 2019. <https://www.nytimes.com/2018/05/16/opinion/college-useful-cost-jobs.html

"*Saban on 60 Minutes.*" Prod. Draggan Mihailovich. 60 Minutes. CBS. New York, 3 Nov. 2013. Television

Scholarship Stats.com. Scholarship Stats.com, 2018. Web. 22 Dec. 2018. <http://www.scholarshipstats.com/scholarshipodds.html>.

Scholarship Stats.com. Scholarship Stats.com, 2018. Web. 22 Dec. 2018. http://www.scholarshipstats.com/about.html>.

Scholarship Stats.com. Scholarship Stats.com, 2018. Web. 22 Dec. 2018. <http://www.scholarshipstats.com/average-per-athlete.html>.

Scholarship Stats.com. Scholarship Stats.com, 2018. Web. 22 Dec. 2018. <http://www.scholarshipstats.com/varsityodds.html>.

Slideroom.com. SlideRoom, 2018. Web. 10 Dec. 2018. <http://www.slideroom.com/>.

Slideroom.com. SlideRoom + The Common Application, 2018. Web. 10 Dec. 2018. <http://www.slideroom.com/commonapp/guide.html>.

Smith-Barrow, Delece. "Apply to the Right Number of Colleges". usnews.com. US New& World Report, 27 Jul. 2017. Web. 2 Feb. 2019. <https://www.usnews.com/education/best-colleges/articles/2017-07-27/how-many-colleges-should-i-apply-to>.

Sports-reference.com. Sports Reference, LLC, 2000-2018. Web. 27 Dec. 2018. <https://www.sports-reference.com/cfb/coaches/nick-saban-1.html>.

Stanford.edu. "Types of Financial Aid." Stanford: Financial Aid. Stanford University, "n.d." Web. 21 Jan. 2019. <https://financialaid.stanford.edu/undergrad/types/index.html>.

Studentaid.ed.gov. Federal Student Aid: An office of the Department of Education, "n.d." Web, 21 Jan. 2019. <https://studentaid.ed.gov/sa/sites/default/files/aid-glance-2018-19.pdf>.

Studentaid.ed.gov. Federal Student Aid: An office of the Department of Education, "n.d." Web. 21 Jan. 2019. <https://studentaid.ed.gov/sa/types/work-study>.

Studentaid.ed.gov. Federal Student Aid: An office of the Department of Education, "n.d." Web. 21 Jan. 2019. <https://studentaid.ed.gov/sa/1920/help/need-parent-info>.

Universalcollegeapp.com. ApplicationsOnline, LLC, 2017-2018. Web. 12 Dec. 2018.
<https://www.universalcollegeapp.com/documents/uca-arts-supplement.pdf>.

Universalcollegeapp.com. ApplicationsOnline, LLC, 2018. Web. 12 Dec. 2018. <https://
www.universalcollegeapp.com/resources#forms>.

Vachon, Ron. Telephone interview. 10 Mar. 2015.

————. Telephone Interview. 18 May 2016.

Wellesley.edu. Wellesley College: Admission and Financial Aid Trustees of Wellesley
College, 2018. Web. 19 Dec. 2018. <https://www.wellesley.edu/admission/esp/
firstyear/decisionplans>.

Wasik, John. "4 Powerful Ways To Find Free College Money". forbes.com,
Forbes, 18, May 2018. Web. 5 Jan. 2019. <https://www.forbes.com/sites/
impactpartners/2019/02/05/risky-assets-in-the-wrong-areas/#d21507c171b8>.

about the author

Terry Greene Clark earned her Bachelor of Science degree in Business Administration from Northeastern University and a Masters in Business Administration from the University of Massachusetts. More recently, she received a certificate in Decorative Arts from Boston Architectural College. She has worked in corporate America and played a role in the start up and organization of a family business where she currently works as an interior designer. Over the past 26 years, she and her husband, Greg, have been raising their four children.

As an outdoor enthusiast, Terry has run several Boston Marathons and participated in a few Hyannis Sprint Triathlons. An integral part of the community, she has been a soccer coach, a Girl Scout leader and a volunteer at numerous school and Boston based nonprofit organizations. Terry founded and ran a community service organization for elementary-aged children for ten years, and she, along with her husband, recently started a nonprofit organization, The Dorchester Foundation. All of these life experiences have nurtured her compassionate nature and desire to share her knowledge and experience with others.

For more information about Terry Greene Clark, go to terrygreeneclark.com.